GS750 FOURS · 1977
SERVICE · REPAIR · PERFORMANCE

By
MIKE BISHOP

ERIC JORGENSEN
Editor

JEFF ROBINSON
Publisher

CLYMER PUBLICATIONS

World's largest publisher of books devoted exclusively to automobiles, motorcycles, and boats.

222 NORTH VIRGIL AVENUE · LOS ANGELES, CALIFORNIA 90004

FIRST EDITION
First Printing February, 1978

Printed in U.S.A.

ଽଉ

ISBN: 0-89287-189-X

MEMBER

MOTORCYCLE INDUSTRY COUNCIL

COVER:
Steve McLaughlin riding the Yoshimura R&D Suzuki GS750
to a record-shattering win in the Superbike Production
class of the 1977 Champion Spark Plug 200 at Laguna Seca.

Photographed by Mike Brown — Visual Imagery,
Los Angeles, California

•

Performance Improvement chapter by Chris Bunch

CONTENTS

CHAPTER ELEVEN

PERFORMANCE IMPROVEMENT 137

QUICK REFERENCE DATA

STATIC TIMING

Cylinders 1 & 4

Cylinders 2 & 3

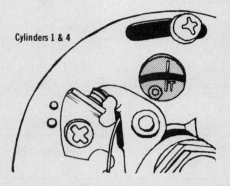
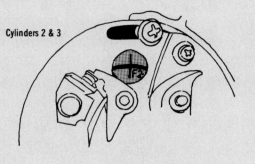

ADVANCED TIMING

Cylinders 1 & 4

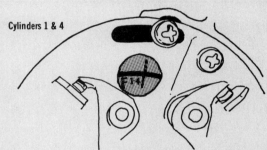

CAM TIMING

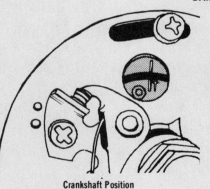
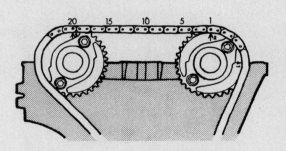

Crankshaft Position

Camshaft Position

IGNITION SPECIFICATIONS

Point gap	0.018 in. (0.35mm)
Spark plug gap	0.024-0.028 in. (0.6-0.7mm)
Spark plug type	NGK B-8ES; ND W24ES
Ignition timing	
Below 1,500 rpm	17° BTDC
Above 2,500 rpm	37° BTDC

CAPACITIES

Fuel tank (includes reserve)	4.8 gal. U.S.; 4 gal. Imp.; 18 liters
Reserve capacity	2.1 gal. U.S.; 8 gal. Imp.; 8 liters
Engine oil (during change)	3.6 U.S.; 3.2 qt. Imp; 3.4 liters (SAE low 40—general use)
Fork oil	180cc each leg (50/50 SAE 10W 30/ATF)

CARBURETION

Idle speed	1,000 rpm
Air screw setting	1 ¼ turns out

VALVES

Tappet clearance	0.0012-0.0031 in. (0.03-0.08mm)
(Intake and exhaust)	

TIRE PRESSURES

Front (solo)	25 psi (1.75 kg^2)
Rear (solo)	28 psi (2.0 kg^2)

—NOTES—

SUZUKI

GS750 FOURS · 1977
SERVICE · REPAIR · PERFORMANCE

CHAPTER ONE

GENERAL INFORMATION

This book provides maintenance and repair information for the Suzuki GS750 motorcycle.

Read the following service hints to make the work as easy and pleasant as possible. Performing your own work can be an enjoyable and rewarding experience.

MANUAL ORGANIZATION

This manual provides detailed service information and procedures for the Suzuki GS 750 motorcycle. All dimensions and capacities are expressed in English units familiar to U.S. mechanics, as well as in metric units. Critical measurements (e.g., piston-to-cylinder clearance, wear limits on brake hydraulic components, etc.) should be made with metric devices; the conversion to English in these cases is not always sufficiently accurate.

This chapter provides general information and specifications. See **Table 1** (found at the end of the chapter). It also discusses equipment and tools useful for both preventive maintenance and troubleshooting.

Chapter Two explains all periodic lubrication and routine maintenance necessary to keep your bike running well. Chapter Two also includes recommended tune-up procedures, eliminating the need to constantly consult chapters on the various subassemblies.

Chapter Three provides methods and suggestions for quick and accurate diagnosis and repair of problems. Troubleshooting procedures discuss typical symptoms and logical methods for pinpointing the trouble.

Subsequent chapters describe specific systems such as the engine, transmission, and electrical system. Each chapter provides disassembly, repair, and assembly procedures in simple step-by-step form. If a repair is impractical for a home mechanic, it is so indicated. It is usually faster and less expensive to take such repairs to a dealer or competent repair shop. Specifications concerning a particular system are included at the end of the appropriate chapter.

Some of the procedures in this manual specify special tools. In all cases, the tool is illustrated either in actual use or alone. A well-equipped mechanic may find that he can substitute similar tools already on hand or fabricate his own.

The terms NOTE, CAUTION, and WARNING have specific meanings in this manual. A NOTE provides additional information to make a step or procedure easier or clearer. Disregarding a NOTE could cause inconvenience, but would not cause damage or personal injury.

A CAUTION emphasizes areas where equipment damage could result. Disregarding a CAUTION could cause permanent mechanical damage; however, personal injury is unlikely.

A WARNING emphasizes areas where personal injury or even death could result from negligence. Mechanical damage may also occur.

WARNINGS *are to be taken seriously.* In some cases serious injury or death has resulted from disregarding similar warnings.

Throughout this manual keep in mind 2 conventions. "Front" refers to the front of the bike. The front of any component, such as the engine, is the end which faces toward the front of the bike. The left and right side refer to a person sitting on the bike facing forward. For example, the shift lever is on the left side. These rules are simple, but even experienced mechanics occasionally become disoriented.

SERVICE HINTS

Most of the service procedures covered are straightforward and can be performed by anyone reasonably handy with tools. It is suggested, however, that you consider your own capabilities carefully before attempting any operation involving major disassembly of the engine.

Some operations, for example, require the use of a press. It would be wiser to have these performed by a shop equipped for such work, than to try to do the job yourself with makeshift equipment. Other procedures require precision measurements. Unless you have the skills and equipment required, it would be better to have a qualified repair shop make the measurements for you.

Repairs go much faster and easier if your machine is clean before you begin work. There are special cleaners for washing the engine and related parts. Just brush or spray on the cleaning solution, let it stand, then rinse it away with a garden hose. Clean all oily or greasy parts with cleaning solvent as you remove them.

WARNING

Never use gasoline as a cleaning agent. It presents an extreme fire hazard. Be sure to work in a well-ventilated area when using cleaning solvent. Keep a fire extinguisher, rated for gasoline fires, handy in any case.

Special tools are required for some repair procedures. These may be purchased from a dealer (or borrowed if you are on good terms with the service department) or may be fabricated by a mechanic or machinist, often at a considerable savings.

Much of the labor charge for repairs made by dealers is for the removal and disassembly of other parts to reach the defective unit. It is frequently possible to perform the preliminary operations yourself and then take the defective unit in to the dealer for repair at considerable savings.

Once you have decided to tackle the job yourself, read the entire section in this manual which pertains to it, making sure you have identified the proper one. Study the illustrations and text until you have a good idea of what is involved in completing the job satisfactorily. If special tools are required, make arrangements to get them before you start. It is frustrating and time-consuming to get partly into a job and then be unable to complete it.

Simple wiring checks can be easily made at home; but knowledge of electronics is almost a necessity for performing tests with complicated electronic testing gear.

During disassembly of parts keep a few general cautions in mind. Force is rarely needed to get things apart. If parts are a tight fit, like a bearing in a case, there is usually a tool made to separate them. Never use a screwdriver to pry apart parts with machined surfaces such as crankcase halves and valve covers. You will mar the surfaces and end up with leaks.

Make diagrams wherever similar-appearing parts are found. For instance, case cover screws are often not the same length. You may think you can remember where everything came from — but mistakes are costly. There is also the possibility you may be sidetracked and not return to work for days or even weeks — in which interval, carefully laid out parts may have become disturbed.

Tag all similar internal parts for location and mark all mating parts for position. Record number and thickness of any shims as they are removed. Small parts such as bolts can be identified by placing them in plastic sandwich bags. Seal and label the bags with masking tape.

Wiring should be tagged with masking tape and marked as each wire is removed. Again, do not rely on memory alone.

Disconnect battery ground cable before working near electrical connections and before disconnecting wires. Never run the engine with the battery disconnected; the alternator could be seriously damaged.

Protect finished surfaces from physical damage or corrosion. Keep gasoline and brake fluid off painted surfaces.

Frozen or very tight bolts and screws can often be loosened by soaking with penetrating oil, then sharply striking the bolt head a few times with a hammer and punch (or screwdriver for screws). Avoid heat, unless absolutely necessary, since it may melt, warp, or remove the temper from many parts.

Avoid flames or sparks when working near a charging battery or flammable liquids such as brake fluid or gasoline.

No parts, except those assembled with a press fit, require unusual force during assembly. If a part is hard to remove or install, find out why before proceeding.

Cover all openings after removing parts to keep dirt, small tools, etc., from falling in.

When assembling 2 parts, start all fasteners, then tighten evenly.

Clutch plates, wiring connections, and brake pads and discs should be kept clean and free of grease and oil.

When assembling parts, be sure all shims and washers are replaced exactly as they came out.

Whenever a rotating part butts against a stationary part, look for a shim or washer. Use new gaskets if there is any doubt about the condition of old ones. Generally you should apply gasket cement to one mating surface only so the parts may be easily disassembled in the future. A thin coat of oil on gaskets helps them seal effectively.

Heavy grease can be used to hold small parts in place if they tend to fall out during assembly. However, keep grease and oil away from electrical components or brake pads and discs.

High spots may be sanded off a piston with sandpaper, but emery cloth and oil do a much more professional job.

Carburetors are best cleaned by disassembling them and soaking the parts in a commercial carburetor cleaner. Never soak gaskets and rubber parts in these cleaners. Never use wire to clean out jets and air passages; they are easily damaged. Use compressed air to blow out the carburetor only if the float has been removed first.

A baby bottle makes a good measuring device for adding oil to forks and transmissions. Get one that is graduated in ounces and cubic centimeters.

Take your time and do the job right. Do not forget that a newly rebuilt motorcycle engine must be broken in the same as a new one. Keep rpm's within the limits given in your owner's manual when you get back on the road.

SAFETY FIRST

Professional motorcycle mechanics can work for years and never sustain a serious injury. If you observe a few rules of common sense and safety, you can enjoy many safe hours servicing your own machine. You could hurt yourself or damage the bike if you ignore these rules.

1. Never use gasoline as a cleaning solvent.

2. Never smoke or use a torch in the vicinity of flammable liquids such as cleaning solvent in open containers.

3. Never smoke or use a torch in an area where batteries are being charged. Highly explosive hydrogen gas is formed during the charging process.

4. If welding or brazing is required on the machine, remove the fuel tank to a safe distance, at least 50 feet away. Welding on gas tanks requires special safety procedures and must be performed by someone skilled in the process.

5. Use the proper sized wrenches to avoid damage to nuts and injury to yourself.

6. When loosening a tight or stuck nut, be guided by what would happen if the wrench should slip. Protect yourself accordingly.

7. Keep your work area clean and uncluttered.

8. Wear safety goggles during all operations involving drilling, grinding, or use of a cold chisel.

9. Never use worn tools.

10. Keep a fire extinguisher handy and be sure it is rated for gasoline and electrical fires.

PARTS REPLACEMENT

Suzuki makes frequent changes during a model year; some minor, some relatively major. When you order parts from the dealer or other parts distributor, always order by engine and chassis number. Write the numbers down and carry them in your wallet. Compare new parts to the old parts before purchasing them. If they are not alike, have the parts manager explain the difference to you.

EXPENDABLE SUPPLIES

Certain expendable supplies are also required. These include grease, oil, gasket cement, wiping rags, cleaning solvent, and distilled water. Ask your dealer for the special locking compounds, silicone lubricants, and commercial chain lube products which make motorcycle maintenance simpler and easier. Solvent is available at most service stations and distilled water for the battery is available at most supermarkets.

TOOLS

For proper servicing, you will need an assortment of ordinary handtools. As a minimum, these include:

a. Metric combination wrenches
b. Metric sockets
c. Plastic mallet
d. Small hammer
e. Snap ring pliers
f. Gas pliers
g. Phillips screwdrivers
h. Slot (common) screwdrivers
i. Feeler gauges
j. Spark plug gauge
k. Spark plug wrench
l. Dial indicator

Engine tune-up and troubleshooting procedures require a few more tools, described in the following sections.

Hydrometer

This instrument measures state of charge of the battery, and tells much about battery condition. Such an instrument is available at any auto parts store and through most larger mail order outlets. A satisfactory one costs less than $3. See **Figure 1**.

Multimeter or VOM

This instrument (**Figure 2**) is invaluable for electrical system troubleshooting and service. A few of its functions may be duplicated by locally fabricated substitutes, but for the serious hobbyist, it is a must. Its uses are described in the applicable sections of this book. Prices start at around $10 at electronics hobbyist stores and mail order outlets.

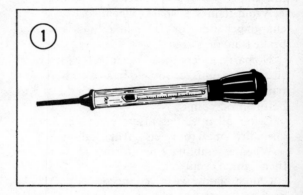

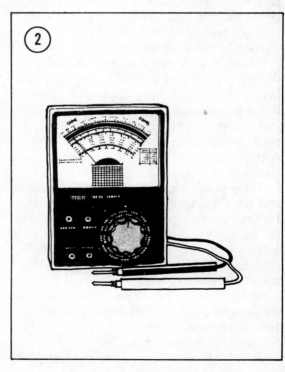

Compression Gauge

An engine with low compression cannot be properly tuned and will not develop full power. A compression gauge measures engine compression. The one shown in **Figure 3** has a flexible stem which enables it to reach cylinders where there is little clearance between the cylinder head and frame. Inexpensive ones start around $3, available at auto accessory stores or by mail order from large catalog order firms.

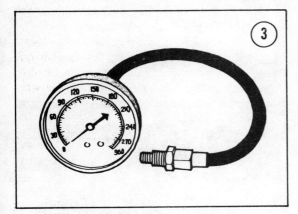

Impact Driver

This tool might have been designed with the motorcyclist in mind. It makes removal of engine cover screws easy, and eliminates damaged screw slots. Good ones run about $12 at larger hardware stores. See **Figure 4**.

Carburetor Gauge Set

A gauge set which can display manifold vacuum for all 4 cylinders simultaneously will greatly simplify carburetor synchronization. **Figure 5** shows the Suzuki gauge set. Less expensive versions are available.

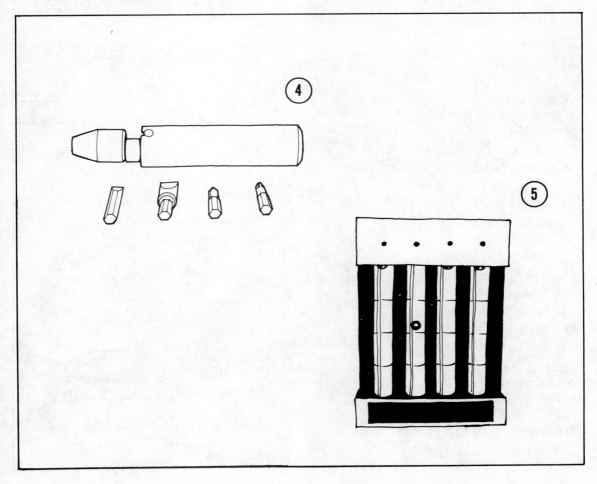

Strobe Timing Light

This instrument is necessary for tuning. It permits very accurate ignition timing by flashing a light at the precise instant cylinder fires. Marks on the ignition advance governor are lined up with the side cover mark while the engine is running.

Suitable lights range from inexpensive neon bulb types ($2-3) to powerful xenon strobe lights ($20-40). See **Figure 6**. Neon timing lights are difficult to see and must be used in dimly lit areas. Xenon strobe timing lights can be used outside in bright sunlight. Both types work on this motorcycle; use according to the manufacturer's instructions.

Other Special Tools

A few other special tools may be required for major service. These are described in the appropriate chapters and are available from Suzuki dealers.

SERIAL NUMBERS

You must know the model serial number for registration purposes and when ordering special parts.

The frame serial number is stamped on the right side of the steering head. See **Figure 7**. The engine serial number is stamped on top of the right crankcase.

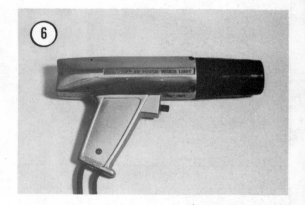

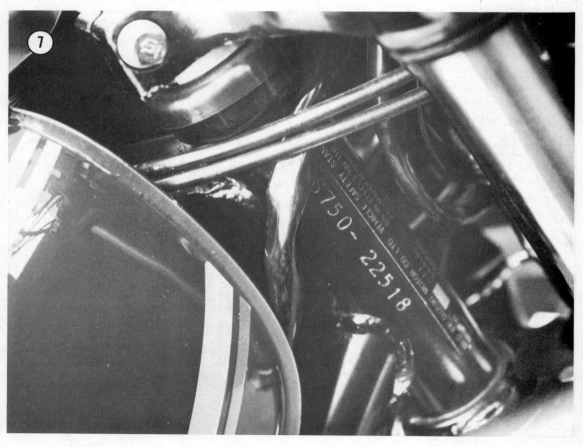

Table 1   GENERAL SPECIFICATIONS

Engine type	4-stroke, DOHC, in-line 4-cylinder
Bore and stroke	65mm x 56.4mm (2.56 in. x 2.22 in.)
Displacement	748cc (45.6 cu. in.)
Compression ratio	8.7:1
Carburetion	4 Mikuni VM26SS
Ignition	Battery and coil
Lubrication	Wet sump, filter and pump
Clutch	Wet, multi-plate
Transmission	5-speed, constant-mesh
Transmission ratios	
1st	2.571
2nd	1.777
3rd	1.380
4th	1.125
5th	0.961
Final drive ratio	2.733
Starting system	Electric and manual kick
Front suspension	Telescopic fork, oil dampened
Rear suspension	Swinging arm, oil-dampened springs
Front tire	3.25H x 19, 4 PR
Rear tire	4.00H x 18, 4 PR
Fuel tank capacity (includes reserve)	18 liters (4.8 U.S. gal.; 4 Imp. gal.)
Reserve capacity	2 liters (2.1 U.S. gal.; 1.8 Imp. gal.)
Engine oil capacity (when changing)	3.4 liters (3.6 U.S. qt.; 3.2 Imp. qt.)
Fork oil capacity (each leg)	180cc (6.04 U.S. oz.; 6.34 Imp. oz.)

1

CHAPTER TWO

PERIODIC LUBRICATION
AND MAINTENANCE

A motorcycle is subjected to tremendous heat, stress, and vibration — even in normal use. When neglected, it will become unreliable and even dangerous to ride. When correctly maintained, the Suzuki GS750 is one of the most reliable motorcycles available and it will provide many years and thousands of miles of trouble-free, fast, and safe riding.

Service intervals are set at 3,000 miles. Lubrication intervals are staggered, depending on the component or system (see **Table 1**). The service interval schedule is shown in **Table 2**.

While time intervals are not provided, a correlation of 500 miles per month provides a good rule of thumb. For example, engine oil change is recommended every 1,500 miles. This approximates 3 months. If you ride less than 500 miles per month the oil should then be changed every 3 months regardless of miles.

If the motorcycle is used primarily in stop-and-go traffic it is a good idea to change the oil more often than is recommended. This is also true for excessive short-haul use. Acids tend to build up rapidly under these conditions and if they are allowed to remain in the engine they will accelerate wear.

This chapter describes all periodic maintenance required to keep the motorcycle running properly. Routine checks are easily performed at each fuel stop. Other periodic maintenance appears in order of frequency. The engine tune-up which must be performed every 3,000 miles is treated separately because the various procedures interact and must be done together and in sequence.

ROUTINE CHECKS

The following simple checks should be carried out at each fuel stop.

Engine Oil Level

Place the motorcycle on the center stand and check the oil level through the inspection window (**Figure 1**). Maintain the level between the F and L marks. Use the appropriate oil recommended in **Table 3**.

General Inspection

1. Examine the engine for signs of oil or fuel leakage.
2. Check the tires for imbedded stones and pry them out with the ignition key.
3. Check all the lights to make sure they work.

NOTE: *At least, always check the stoplight. Motorists can't stop as quickly as you can and they need all the warning you can give them.*

Table 1   LUBRICATION INTERVALS

	Initial 1,000 Km (750 miles)	Initial and Every 2,500 Km (1,500 miles)	Initial and Every 5,000 Km (3,000 miles)	Initial and Every 10,000 Km (6,000 miles)
Drive chain	Every 1,000 Km (750 miles)			
Throttle cable			Motor oil	Motor oil
Throttle grip				Grease
Contact breaker cam oil felt			Motor oil	Motor oil
Wheel bearings	Grease every 2 years or 20,000 Km (12,000 miles)			
Speedometer gear housing				
Steering stem bearings				
Swinging arm				
Engine oil	Change	Change	Change	Change
Front fork oil	Change			Change
Clutch cable			Motor oil	Motor oil
Brake pedal			Grease or oil	Grease or oil

Table 2   SERVICE INTERVALS

	Initial 1,000 Km (750 miles)	Initial and Every 5,000 Km (3,000 miles)	Initial and Every 10,000 Km (6,000 miles)
Oil filter	Change	Change	Change
Carburetor	Adjust	Adjust	Adjust
Contact breaker point and timing	Check and adjust	Check and adjust	Check and adjust
Spark plug	Clean and adjust gap	Clean and adjust gap	Replace
Air cleaner element		Clean	Clean
Clutch	Adjust	Adjust	Adjust
Exhaust pipe and muffler	Retighten	Retighten	Retighten
Compression	Check	Check	Check
Oil pressure		Check	Check
Oil sump filter			Clean
Tappet clearance	Check	Check	Check
Drive chain	Adjust every 1,000 km (750 miles)		
Battery	Check	Check	Check
Brake system (front and rear)	Check	Check	Check
Throttle cable	Adjust	Adjust	Adjust
Tire		Check	Check
Fuel hose	Change every 2 years		
Brake hose			
Steering	Check	Check	Check
All nuts and bolts (engine and body)	Retighten	Retighten	Retighten

Table 3   RECOMMENDED OIL

Viscosity	Temperature Range
SAE 10W	$-4°$ to $32°F$ ($-20°$ to $0°C$)
SAE 20W	$14°$ to $60°F$ ($-10°$ to $15°C$)
SAE 10W-30	$-4°$ to $86°F$ ($-20°$ to $30°C$)
SAE 10W-50	$-4°F$ ($-20°C$) and over
SAE 20W-50	$14°F$ ($-10°C$) and over
SAE 30	$60°$ to $86°F$ ($15°$ to $30°C$)
SAE 40	$86°F$ ($30°C$) and over

4. Check the drive chain. Although it is permanently lubricated internally, it should also have a light external coat of engine oil (**Figure 2**).

CAUTION
Do not use specially compounded chain oil on the drive chain. While most of the oils available are excellent for standard chains, penetrants they might contain could attack the O-ring seals around the pins and permit the permanent lubrication to become thinned or contaminated, resulting in decreased chain life.

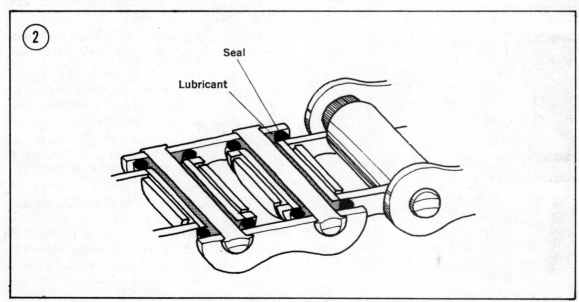

Seal

Lubricant

2

Tire Pressure

Tire pressure must be checked with the tires cold. Correct tire pressure depends on load. See **Table 4**.

Battery

Raise the seat and check the electrolyte level in the battery. The level must be between the upper and lower level marks on the case. If the level is low, top it up with distilled water only; never add electrolyte to a battery that has been in service.

Table 4   TIRE PRESSURE

	Under 200 lb. Load	Over 200 lb. Load
Normal riding		
Front	25 psi (1.75 kg^2)	25 psi (1.75 kg^2)
Rear	28 psi (2.0 kg^2)	32 psi (2.25 kg^2)
Sustained high-speed riding		
Front	28 psi (2.0 kg^2)	28 psi (2.0 kg^2)
Rear	32 psi (2.25 kg^2)	36 psi (2.5 kg^2)

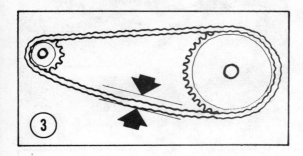

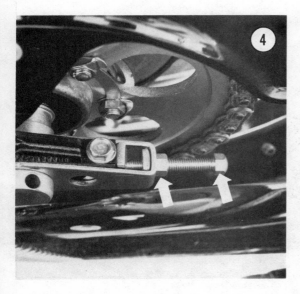

PERIODIC MAINTENANCE

The following procedures are summarized in **Tables 1 and 2**.

Engine tune-up procedures, all of which should be done every 3,000 miles, are correctly called preventive maintenance. However, the procedures should be done together, and in a specific sequence for best results. For this reason, the procedures are grouped under the heading Engine *Tune-up*.

750-MILE SERVICE

Only one item need be serviced every 750 miles — the drive chain. This service is very important. Accelerated drive chain wear growing out of neglect can prove very costly. And drive chain failure, particularly at high speed where it is most likely to occur, cannot only prove very costly, but it may be disastrous and fatal as well. At the least, a failed chain could severely damage the engine and transmission. At the worst, it could foul the rear sprocket and lock the rear wheel.

1. Check the slack in the chain, midway on the bottom run (**Figure 3**). It should be ¾-1 in. (20-25mm).

2. To adjust the chain, loosen the axle nut and the adjuster locknuts on each side (**Figure 4**). Turn the adjuster bolts in (to tighten the chain) or out (to loosen the chain) equally.

3. Check the alignment of the wheels as described below and correct it if necessary. Then tighten the rear axle nut to 60-80 ft.-lb. (8.3-11.0 mkg).

4. Soak a clean shop rag in engine oil, wrap it around the chain and hold it in place, and slowly turn the rear wheel to allow the chain to run through the rag until the entire chain has been coated with a light film of oil. Refer to the CAUTION following Step 4, *Routine Maintenance*.

5. Inspect the drive sprockets and replace them if they show signs of wear and undercutting (**Figure 5**). See Chapter Nine for rear sprocket replacement and Chapter Four for drive sprocket replacement.

3,000-MILE SERVICE

Throttle Cables

The throttle cables should have $^1/_{64}$-$^1/_{32}$ in. (1-1.5mm) free play. If adjustment is necessary, loosen the locknuts (**Figure 6**) and turn the adjuster in or out to achieve the correct free play. Then tighten the locknuts.

The throttle cables should be oiled every 3,000 miles. Remove the screws from the switch and throttle case (**Figure 7**). Disconnect the cables from the throttle and attach a cable lubricator (**Figure 8**). This is the only certain method of ensuring complete lubrication. (There are several lubricators available through dealers.) Force lubricant through the cable until it runs out the other end, then reconnect the cables and adjust them as described above.

Clutch Cable

The clutch cable should be adjusted so there is $^5/_{32}$ in. (4mm) of free play at the lever base (**Figure 9**).

1. Loosen the locknut and screw the cable adjuster all the way into the clutch lever bracket.

2. Remove the clutch adjuster cover. Loosen the locknut 2 or 3 turns. Run in the adjuster until there is resistance. Then loosen the adjuster ¼ turn, hold it to prevent it from turning further, and tighten the locknut. See **Figure 10**.

3. Install the cover and adjust the free play of the lever.

4. Road test the motorcycle to make sure the clutch fully engages and disengages.

Brake Pedal

Lightly oil the rear brake pedal pivot shaft, working the oil in by moving the lever up and down.

Brake Lines

Check the brake lines between the master cylinders and the calipers. If there is any leakage, tighten the connections or replace leaking lines and hoses and fill and bleed the system as described in Chapter Ten.

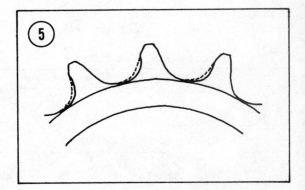

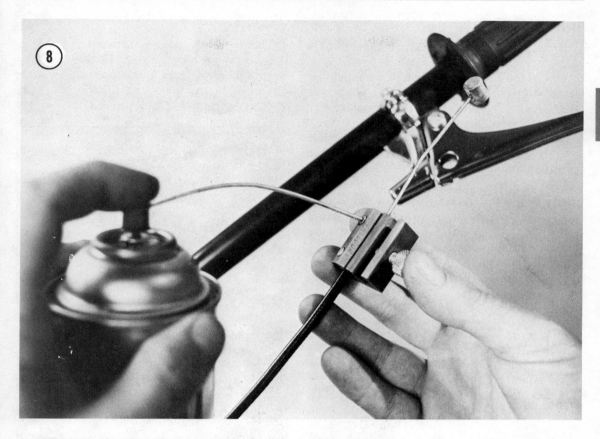

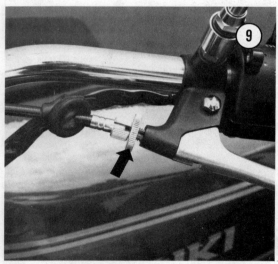

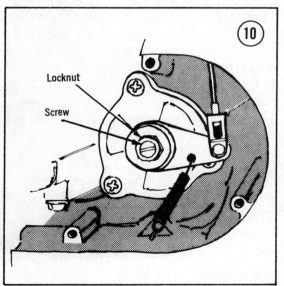

Brake Fluid Level

Check the level in both the front and rear brake master cylinder reservoirs (**Figures 11 and 12**). Maintain the level between the upper and lower marks on the reservoir.

WARNING
Use brake fluid clearly marked DOT 3 and/or SAE J1703 only. Others may vaporize and cause brake failure.

Brake Pad Inspection

Brake pad wear depends on a number of factors including riding conditions and rider habits. If most of your riding is in mountainous areas, stop-and-go traffic, or if you know you are heavy on the brakes, check them more frequently than recommended here.

To check the pads remove the inspection cover from the rear caliper (**Figure 13**) and look to see if either or both pads are worn down to the red limit line. The front pads are checked in the same manner, although there is no inspection cover to remove. If either pad in either caliper is worn down to the line, replace the pads in that caliper as a set (see Chapter Ten).

Tires

Check tire tread for excessive wear, deep cuts, imbedded objects such as stones, glass, nails, etc. If you find a nail in a tire, mark its location with a light crayon or chalk before pulling it out; this will help you locate the hole in the inner tube.

Check local traffic regulations concerning minimum tread depth. Measure with a tread depth gauge or small rule (**Figure 14**). Tires should be replaced when the tread depth is less than $1/16$ in. (1.5mm) — front; $3/32$ in. (2mm) — rear.

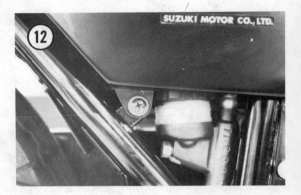

Exhaust System

Tighten the head pipe collar nuts at the cylinder head. Tighten the head pipe-to-muffler clamp bolts and the muffler mounting bolts.

Steering

Check the steering for play and adjust it if necessary as described in Chapter Eight, *Steering Head Adjustment*.

6,000-MILE SERVICE

Throttle Grip

Loosen the screws in the throttle and switch housing (**Figure 15**) but do not remove them. Remove the throttle cable clamp from the handlebar, slide the throttle back, and clean the bar with solvent and then dry it. Apply a light coat

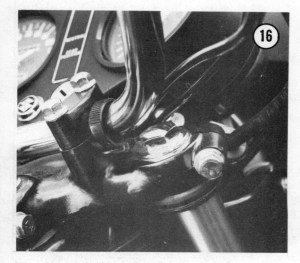

2

of grease to the bar. Slide the throttle back into position and tighten the screws. Install a cable clamp and check the action of the throttle. It should turn freely and snap back when released.

Front Fork Oil

The front fork oil should be changed every 6,000 miles.

1. Wrap several shop rags over the top of the fuel tank and tape them in place. Remove the handlebars and place them on the tank.

2. Unscrew the fork cap nuts (**Figure 16**).

3. Place a drip pan beneath one of the fork legs and unscrew the drain plug (**Figure 17**). Allow several minutes for the oil to drain. Then reinstall the drain plug and drain the other fork leg in the same manner.

4. Mix approximately 200cc of SAE 10W/30 oil with 200cc of ATF.

5. With a funnel, fill each fork leg with 180cc of the mixture. Fill the legs slowly; the oil must have time to migrate down through the springs. If oil is added too quickly, it will spill out over the top of the fork leg making it impossible to fill it accurately.

6. When both legs have been filled, install the cap nuts and the handlebars.

Oil Sump Filter

The oil sump filter should be cleaned at every other oil change.

1. After the sump and filter cavity have been drained, unscrew the bolts that attach the sump to the bottom of the engine (**Figure 18**).

2. Remove the pickup screen from the pump. Clean both the screen and the sump with solvent and dry them.

3. Install the screen. Install the sump and tighten the bolts in the pattern shown in **Figure 19**.

Engine Oil and Filter Change

Periodic and timely oil change will contribute more to engine longevity than any other single factor. Change oil every 3,000 miles or more often in dusty areas or if the motorcycle is used primarily in short-haul trips.

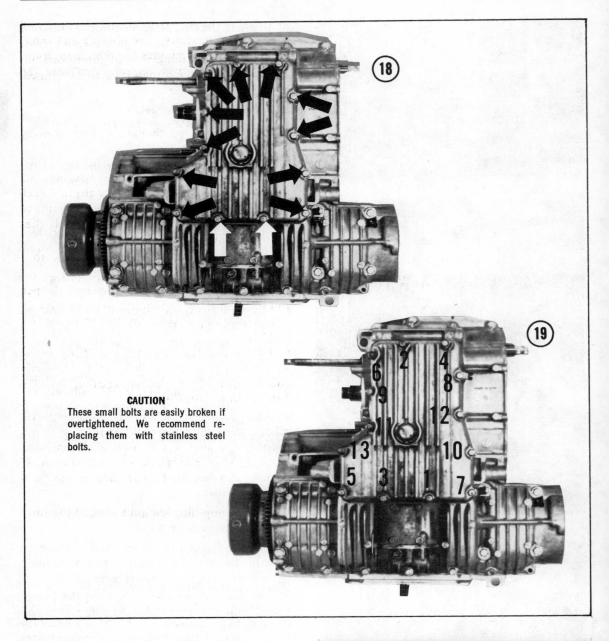

CAUTION
These small bolts are easily broken if overtightened. We recommend replacing them with stainless steel bolts.

1. Warm up the engine. Set the motorcycle on the centerstand.

2. Remove the oil filler cap (**Figure 20**).

3. Place a drip pan beneath the engine and unscrew the drain plug (**Figure 21**).

> WARNING
> *Get your hand out of the way as soon as the plug is ready to come out. Hot oil drains rapidly and could cause painful burns.*

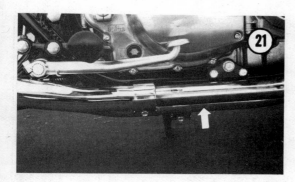

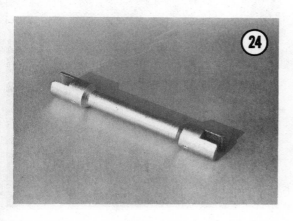

4. Unscrew the nuts from the oil filter housing (**Figure 22**) and remove the housing and filter. Allow at least 10 minutes for the oil to drain. Turn the engine over several times with the kickstarter.

CAUTION
Do not allow the engine to start or it will be damaged.

5. Clean the oil drain bolt, filter housing, and filter cavity with solvent and dry them. Check the gasket on the bolt and the housing O-ring to make sure they are in good condition. If they are not, replace them.

6. Install the drain bolt and tighten it to 1 mkg (7.2 ft.-lb.).

7. Install a new filter in the filter cavity, open end in. Install the spring and housing with O-ring (**Figure 23**). Tighten the nuts to 1 mkg (7.2 ft.-lb.).

8. Fill the crankcase through the filler opening with 3.6 U.S. quarts (3.4 liters; 3.2 Imperial quarts) of the appropriate grade of oil shown in **Table 3**. Install the filler plug.

9. Start the engine and allow it to idle so the oil will completely circulate. When the engine has warmed up, shut it off, wait a minute, and check the level through the oil level window. If the level is below the L mark, add oil until it is correct.

10. Check carefully for leaks around the filter housing and the drain plug.

Wheels, Hubs, Rims, and Spokes

Check wheel hubs and rims for bends and other signs of damage. Check both wheels for broken or bent spokes. Replace damaged ones immediately. See Chapters Eight and Nine. Tap each spoke lightly with a small hammer or wrench. All spokes should emit the same sound. A spoke that is too tight will have a higher pitch than the others; one that is too loose will have a lower pitch. If only one or two spokes are slightly out of adjustment, adjust them with a spoke wrench (**Figure 24**). If more are affected, the wheel should be removed and trued. See *Spoke Adjustment*, Chapter Eight.

Front Suspension Check

1. Lock the front brake and pump the forks up and down as vigorously as possible. The suspension should operate smoothly and without play.

2. Check and tighten the top and bottom fork pinch bolts (**Figures 25A and 25B**).

3. Check and tighten the handlebar mounting bolts (**Figure 26**).

4. Check and tighten the axle cap bolts and the axle nut (**Figure 27**).

5. Check and tighten the caliper mounting bolts (**Figure 28**).

Rear Suspension Check

1. Check and tighten rear axle nut (**Figure 29**).

2. Check and tighten the swing arm pivot bolt (**Figure 30**).

3. Check and tighten the suspension unit mounting bolts (**Figure 31**).

Nuts, Bolts, and Other Fasteners

Constant vibration can loosen many fasteners on a motorcycle. Every 6,000 miles check the tightness of *all* fasteners, particularly those on:

a. Engine mounts
b. Engine covers
c. Handlebars
d. Gearshift lever
e. Exhaust system
f. Brake system
g. Lighting equipment

12,000-MILE SERVICE

The 12,000-mile service consists of all of the items required during 6,000-mile service plus the following.

Wheel Bearings

The wheel bearings should be checked, cleaned, and greased as described in Chapters Eight and Nine.

Speedometer Drive

The speedometer drive (**Figure 32**) should be removed, cleaned, and greased when the front wheel bearings are serviced.

EVERY 2 YEARS

Every 2 years the fuel and brake hoses should be routinely replaced and the brake systems should be drained and filled with fresh fluid (see Chapter Ten).

ENGINE TUNE-UP

An engine tune-up consists of several accurate and careful adjustments made in order to obtain maximum engine performance. Because different systems in an engine interact to affect overall performance, tune-up must be carried out in the following order:

   a. Valve clearance adjustment

   b. Ignition adjustment and timing

   c. Carburetor adjustment

Perform an engine tune-up every 3,000 miles. During every other tune-up, expendable ignition parts (spark plugs, condensers, contact breakers) should be replaced.

Table 5 summarizes tune-up specifications.

Table 5   TUNE-UP SPECIFICATIONS

Valves	
Tappet clearance (intake and exhaust)	0.0012-0.0031 in. (0.03-0.08mm)
Ignition	
Contact breaker gap	0.018 in. (0.35mm)
Spark plug	
Type	NGK B-8ES; ND W24ES
Gap	0.024-0-0.028 in. (0.6-0.7mm)
Timing	
Below 1,500 rpm	17° BTDC
Above 2,500 rpm	37° BTDC
Carburetion	
Idle speed	1,000 rpm
Air screw setting	1¼ turns out

Checking Valve Clearance

Valve clearance should be checked with the engine cold. If the clearance is incorrect, it must be adjusted; if the clearance is too small, the valves may be burned or distorted. If it is too large, the valve train will be noisy and performance will be poor.

1. Set the motorcycle on the centerstand. Remove the seat.

2. Disconnect the high-tension leads from the spark plugs and unscrew them from the cylinder head. Note their locations, by cylinder number, for reference later on.

3. Disconnect the cam cover breather hose (**Figure 33**).

4. Remove the cam end covers (**Figure 34**).

5. Unscrew the bolts that attach the cam cover. Note the location of the high-tension lead retaining clips on the rear bolts on either end (**Figure 35**). Tap around the sealing surface of the cover with a soft mallet to break it loose and remove it.

6. Remove the contact breaker cover to expose the breaker cam bolt in the right end of the crankshaft (**Figure 36**) this bolt (17mm) will be used to rotate the crankshaft and camshafts during clearance check.

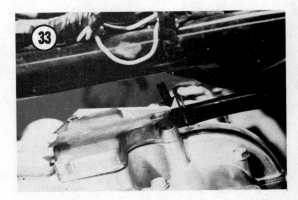

7. Rotate the crankshaft clockwise to bring the No. 1 exhaust cam to the position shown in **Figure 37**. Check the clearance of No. 1 and No. 2 exhaust tappets. The clearance should be 0.03-0.08mm (0.0012-0.0030 in.). Write down the actual clearance and proceed with the next three steps.

8. Rotate the crankshaft 180° to bring the No. 1 intake cam to the position shown in **Figure 38**. Check the clearance of the No. 1 and No. 2 intake tappets. Write down the actual clearance.

9. Rotate the crankshaft 180° to bring the No. 4 exhaust cam to the position shown in **Figure 39**. Check the clearance of the No. 3 and No. 4 exhaust tappets. Write down the actual clearance.

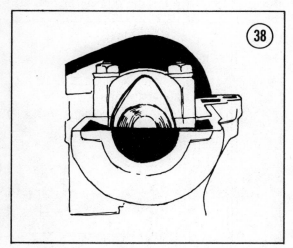

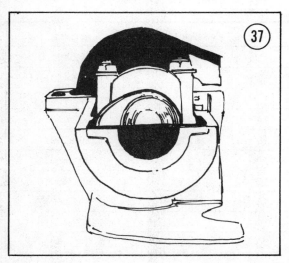

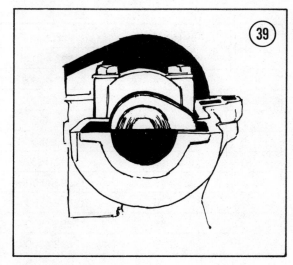

10. Rotate the crankshaft 180° to bring the No. 4 intake cam to the position shown in **Figure 40**. Check the clearance of the No. 3 and No. 4 intake tappets. Write down the actual clearance.

Adjusting Valve Clearance

The recommended valve clearance of 0.03-0.08mm (0.0012-0.0030 in.) should be maintained for all valves. Valve clearance is adjusted and controlled by shims set in the top of each tappet. The range of shims available, along with their part numbers, is shown in **Table 6**.

Before replacing any of the shims to correct clearance, determine the actual shims that are required. To do this, use the special tappet depresser (Suzuki part No. 09916-64510) (**Figure 41**) to depress the tappet (**Figure 42**).

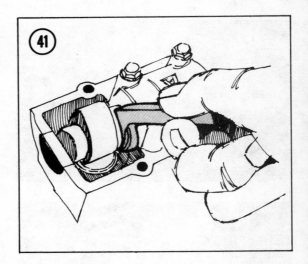

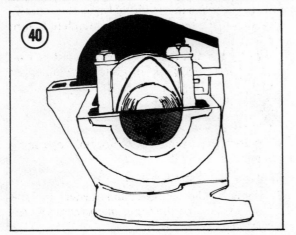

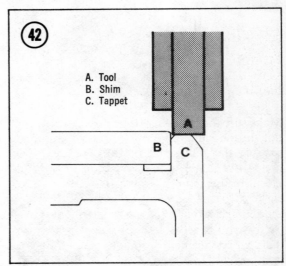

A. Tool
B. Shim
C. Tappet

Table 6   TAPPET SHIM SIZES

No.	Thickness (mm)	Part No.	No.	Thickness	Part No.
1	2.15	12892-45000	11	2.65	12892-45010
2	2.20	12892-45001	12	2.70	12892-45011
3	2.25	12892-45002	13	2.75	12892-45012
4	2.30	12892-45003	14	2.80	12892-45013
5	2.35	12892-45004	15	2.85	12892-45014
6	2.40	12892-45005	16	2.90	12892-45015
7	2.45	12892-45006	17	2.95	12892-45016
8	2.50	12892-45007	18	3.00	12892-45017
9	2.55	12892-45008	19	3.05	12892-45018
10	2.60	12892-45009	20	3.10	12892-45019

Make sure the depresser bears on the tappet and not on the shim. Press down on the tool and remove the tappet shim with tweezers (**Figure 43**). Write the number (size) of the shim adjacent to the actual clearance number recorded earlier. Do this for all of the cylinders for which the actual clearance was out of specification.

Now you're ready to begin calculating the individual replacement shim sizes. The following is a typical example.

Actual No. 1 intake valve clearance	0.10mm (0.0039 in.)
Desired clearance (maximum)	0.08mm (0.0031 in.)
Difference (too large)	0.02mm (0.0008 in.)
Existing shim size	2.45mm (0.0965 in.)

The clearance in this case is at least 0.02mm (0.0008 in.) too large. It must be reduced by at least that amount, through the substitution of a thicker shim. **Table 6** indicates that the next larger shim, No. 8, is 2.50mm (0.098 in.). This shim would reduce the clearance by 0.05mm (0.0020 in.); the clearance would then be 0.05mm (0.0020 in.), well within the specified range.

Calculate all of the required shim sizes for the out-of-specification cylinders in the manner just described. Before purchasing all new shims, check to see if any of the shims that were removed will work on other valves; it is just possible that one, or several, might work and save some expense.

When installing the shims, oil both sides before setting them in place. Recheck the clearances when through, as described earlier, to ensure that they are all correct. Then reinstall the cam box cover.

Compression Test

Every 3,000 miles, check the cylinder compression. Record the results and compare them at the next 3,000-mile check. A running record will show trends in deterioration so that corrective action can be taken before complete failure occurs.

Both a dry test and a wet test should be carried out to isolate the trouble in cylinders or valves.

Dry Test

1. Warm the engine to normal operating temperature.

2. Remove the spark plugs.

3. Connect the compression tester to one cylinder following the tester manufacturer's instructions.

4. Check to make sure the chokes are open. With assistance, hold the throttle fully open and crank the engine until the gauge needle ceases to rise. Record the result. Remove the tester.

5. Repeat Steps 3 and 4 for each cylinder.

When interpreting the results, actual readings are not as important as the differences between readings. All readings should be 128-170 psi (9-12 kg/cm²). Readings below 100 psi (7 kg/cm²) indicate that an engine overhaul is due. A maximum difference of 21 psi (1.5 kg/cm²) between any 2 cylinders is acceptable. Greater differences indicate worn or broken rings, leaky or sticky valves, or a combination of these. To isolate the cause, carry out a wet compression test.

Wet Test

The wet test is carried out in the same way as the dry test; however, before checking a cylinder, pour about an ounce of oil into the cylinder through the spark plug hole, crank the engine several times to distribute the oil on the cylinder walls, and then check the compression as described above.

If the compression in a cylinder increases during the wet test over that indicated in the dry test, the rings and/or bore can be assumed to be worn, or a compression ring may be broken.

If the compression during the wet test does not increase, the trouble is in the valve train.

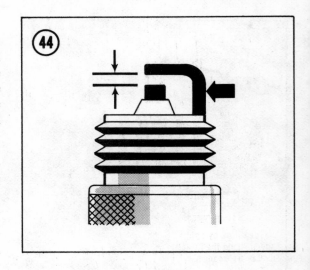

Spark Plug Cleaning/Replacement

1. Grasp the high-tension leads by the spark plug caps and pull them off; never pull on the lead itself.

2. Blow away any dirt that may have accumulated in the spark plug wells with compressed air.

WARNING
Wear safety glasses or goggles when doing this to prevent particles from getting in your eyes.

3. Remove the spark plugs with a spark plug wrench.

NOTE: *If plugs are difficult to remove, apply penetrating oil around the base of the plugs and allow it to soak in for 10-20 minutes.*

4. Inspect the spark plugs carefully. Check for broken or cracked porcelain, excessively eroded electrodes, and excessive carbon or oil fouling. If deposits are light, the plugs may be cleaned in solvent with a wire brush or with a special spark plug sandblast cleaner.

5. Use a wire feeler gauge and gap the plugs to 0.024-0.028 in. (0.6-0.7mm) by bending the side electrode (**Figure 44**). Do not file the electrodes to correct the gap.

6. Install the plugs with *new* gaskets. First apply a *small* drop of oil to the plug threads. Screw the plugs in finger-tight, then tighten an additional ¼ turn. If you must reuse the old gaskets, tighten the plugs only an additional ⅛ turn.

NOTE: *Do not overtighten. This will squash the gaskets and destroy their ability to seal.*

Reading Spark Plugs

Much information about engine condition and spark plug performance can be learned by careful examination of the spark plugs. This information is valid only after performing the following steps.

1. Ride the motorcycle up an incline at full throttle for a short distance in 2nd or 3rd gear to place a load on the engine.

2. Simultaneously pull in the clutch and shut the engine off with the kill switch with the throttle open. Coast to a stop or stop the motorcycle with the brakes; do not use compression to slow the motorcycle.

3. Remove the spark plugs, examine them, and compare them to **Figure 45**.

Contact Breaker Inspection and Cleaning

Through normal use, contacts gradually pit and burn. If this condition is not too serious, they can be dressed with a few strokes of a point file. Do not use emery cloth or sandpaper; they tend to round the contacts, and abrasive particles will remain on them, causing arcing and burning. If the contacts cannot be smoothed with just a few strokes, replace them.

2

SPARK PLUG CONDITION ⓐ45

NORMAL

- Identified by light tan or gray deposits on the firing tip.
- Can be cleaned.

GAP BRIDGED

- Identified by deposit buildup closing gap between electrodes.
- Caused by oil or carbon fouling. If deposits are not excessive, the plug can be cleaned.

OIL FOULED

- Identified by wet black deposits on the insulator shell bore electrodes.
- Caused by excessive oil entering combustion chamber through worn rings and pistons, excessive clearance between valve guides and stems, or worn or loose bearings. Can be cleaned. If engine is not repaired, use a hotter plug.

CARBON FOULED

- Identified by black, dry fluffy carbon deposits on insulator tips, exposed shell surfaces and electrodes.
- Caused by too cold a plug, weak ignition, dirty air cleaner, too rich a fuel mixture, or excessive idling. Can be cleaned.

LEAD FOULED

- Identified by dark gray, black, yellow, or tan deposits or a fused glazed coating on the insulator tip.
- Caused by highly leaded gasoline. Can be cleaned.

WORN

- Identified by severely eroded or worn electrodes.
- Caused by normal wear. Should be replaced.

FUSED SPOT DEPOSIT

- Identified by melted or spotty deposits resembling bubbles or blisters.
- Caused by sudden acceleration. Can be cleaned.

OVERHEATING

- Identified by a white or light gray insulator with small black or gray brown spots and with bluish-burnt appearance of electrodes.
- Caused by engine overheating, wrong type of fuel, loose spark plugs, too hot a plug, or incorrect ignition timing. Replace the plug.

PREIGNITION

- Identified by melted electrodes and possibly blistered insulator. Metallic deposits on insulator indicate engine damage.
- Caused by wrong type of fuel, incorrect ignition timing or advance, too hot a plug, burned valves, or engine overheating. Replace the plug.

If the contacts are still serviceable after filing, remove all residue with lacquer thinner or special contact breaker cleaner. Close the contacts on a strong piece of clean, white paper, such as a business card. Pull the card through the closed contacts until no particles or discoloration remain on the card. Finally, rotate the crankshaft and observe the contacts as they open and close. If they do not meet squarely, replace them.

Adjust the contact gap and ignition timing as described below.

Contact Breaker Replacement

If the contacts are badly damaged, replace them and adjust the gap as described below.

1. Remove the contact breaker cover (**Figure 46**).

2. Unscrew the 2 screws that attach each contact set to the backing plate (**Figure 47**).

3. Loosen the screw in each electrical contact post and disconnect the leads. Remove the condensers; they should be routinely replaced with the contact breakers.

4. Installation is the reverse of these steps.

5. Adjust the contact gap and ignition timing.

Contact Gap Adjustment

The contacts should be inspected every 3,000 miles, and if their condition is good, they can be cleaned and adjusted. If they are badly pitted, replace and adjust them as described below.

1. Remove the contact breaker cover. See **Figure 46**.

2. Rotate the crankshaft clockwise until the No. 1-4 contacts are fully open. Loosen the screws that attach the contact set to the baseplate and set the gap at 0.35mm (0.014 in.). Then tighten the screws without further moving the contacts.

3. Rotate the crankshaft clockwise and align the "F 1-4" on the advance plate with the stationary timing mark (**Figure 48**).

4. Connect a circuit tester or lamp to the positive contact terminal and to ground (**Figure 49**).

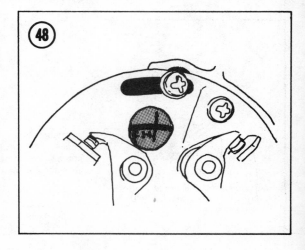

5. Slightly loosen the 3 screws in the ignition baseplate (**Figure 50**). Slowly rotate the plate counterclockwise until the points just begin to open (the lamp will go out). Tighten the screws. Rock the crankshaft back and forth and recheck the timing position with the lamp.

6. Rotate the crankshaft 180° to align the "F 2-3" on the advance plate with the stationary timing mark (**Figure 51**).

7. Connect the tester or lamp to the other contact breaker and check the contact opening point as for the other set. If adjustment is required, loosen the screws in the half-plate (**Figure 52**) and move the plate counterclockwise until the point opening coincides with alignment of the timing marks. Then tighten the screws and recheck to make certain the plate did not move.

Ignition Timing

1. Remove the ignition cover (**Figure 53**).

2. Connect a timing light to the No. 1 cylinder in accordance with the light manufacturer's instructions.

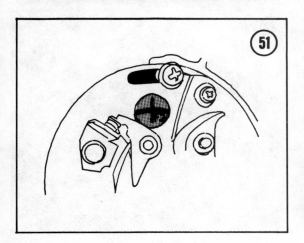

3. Start the engine and run it at varying speeds up to 1,500 rpm, but not higher. Direct the timing light at the timing marks. If the timing is correct, the F mark and the stationary timing mark should align. If not, slight adjustment of the ignition base plate and contact breaker plates is required (see *Contact Gap Adjustment* above).

4. Increase the engine speed to 2,500 rpm and once again check the timing with the light. The advance mark and the stationary mark should now align (**Figure 54**). If not, slight adjustment of the ignition baseplate and contact breaker plates is required.

5. When the No. 1-4 cylinder pair has been checked and timed, connect the light to the No. 2 cylinder and check the No. 2-3 pair.

Air Cleaner

The air cleaner should be cleaned and reoiled every 3,000 miles. It should be done in conjunction with an engine tune-up to ensure that the engine is breathing well so that carburetor adjustments will be correct.

1. Remove the filter cover (**Figure 55**).

2. Unscrew the screw that holds the filter in place and remove the filter element (**Figure 56**).

3. Remove the foam from the filter frame and wash it with clean solvent. Squeeze it as dry as possible; *don't twist it.*

> WARNING
> *Gasoline is a dangerous solvent. Keep flames, heat, and smoking materials out of the area when using gasoline as a solvent. Work in a well-ventilated area, preferably out of doors. Keep a fire extinguisher on hand — one that is rated for gasoline fires. When you are done with the gasoline, place it in a sealable container and cap it tightly.*

4. Soak the filter in motor oil and then squeeze out the excess.

5. Reinstall the filter, making certain it is seated on the filter frame.

Carburetor Adjustment

All the preceding steps under *Engine Tune-Up* must be carried out before the carburetors can be satisfactorily adjusted.

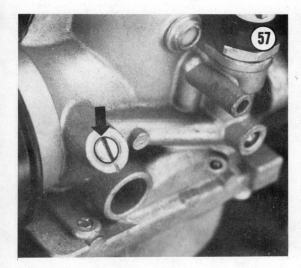

2

1. Screw in the air screw on each carburetor until it bottoms out. Be careful not to over-tighten and strip the threads. Back each screw out 1¼ turns. This is the basic setting. See **Figure 57**.

2. Start the engine and adjust its idle speed at 1,000 rpm with the throttle stop screw (**Figure 58**).

**Carburetor Balancing
(Synchronization)**

Carburetor balancing, or synchronization, is essential for maximum performance. A special gauge, called a manometer, is required to do this job accurately. The one shown here is from Suzuki (part No. 09913-13120). There are others on the market that work equally as well with virtually the same procedure that is described.

1. Before beginning work, the gauge must be calibrated; this must be done each time the gauge is used. Unscrew the 4mm Allen bolt from the intake of the No. 4 carburetor (**Figure 59**). Screw in one of the balancer adapters. Connect the first hose of the balancer to the adapter.

2. Start the engine and run it at a steady 1,500 rpm.

3. Turn the air screw for the tube that is connected until the steel ball lines up with the center mark on the tube (see **Figure 60**).

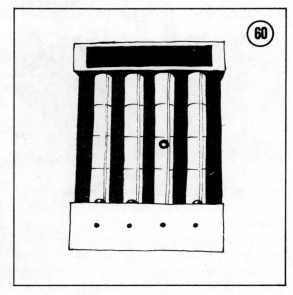

4. Do this for the other tubes in turn until they are all calibrated the same.

5. Unscrew the Allen bolts from the other 3 carburetors, screw in the adapters, and connect the hoses from the gauge.

6. Start the engine and run it at a steady 1,500 rpm. The ball in the tube connected to the No. 4 cylinder should be at the center mark. Likewise, all of the other balls should line up with the center mark and the No. 4 ball. If any of the balls are not lined up with the center mark, proceed with the next steps.

7. Remove the cap from the carburetor that is to be adjusted.

8. Loosen the locknut on the slide lifter adjusting screw (**Figure 61**). Turn the screw as required to bring the ball into line with the center mark. Then, without further turning the screw, tighten the locknut. Install the carburetor cover.

9. Repeat the above for any carburetors that are out of synchronization. When the job is finished, disconnect the balancer gauge, unscrew the adapters, and screw in the Allen bolts, making sure each is fitted with a good washer; air leaks at the inlet tube could cause serious engine damage.

STORAGE

Several months of inactivity can cause serious problems and general deterioration of your bike. This is especially important in areas with extremely cold winters. During the winter, you should prepare your bike carefully for "hibernation."

Selecting a Storage Area

Most cyclists store their bikes in their home garage. If you do not have a garage, there are other facilities for rent or lease in most areas. When selecting an area, consider the following points.

1. The storage area must be dry; there should be no dampness or excessive humidity. A heated area is not necessary, but it should be insulated to minimize extreme temperature variations.

2. Avoid buildings with large window areas. If this is not possible, mask the window to keep direct sunlight off the bike.

3. Avoid buildings in industrial areas where factories are liable to emit corrosive fumes. Also avoid buildings near large bodies of salt water.

4. Select an area where there is minimum risk of fire, theft, or vandalism. Check with your insurance agent to make sure that your insurance covers the bike where it is stored.

Preparing Bike for Storage

Careful preparation will minimize deterioration and make it easier to restore the bike to service later. Use the following procedure.

1. Wash the bike completely. Make certain to remove any road salt which may have accumulated during the first weeks of winter. Wax all painted and polished surfaces, including any chromed areas.

2. Run the engine for 20-30 minutes to stabilize oil temperature. Drain oil, regardless of mileage since last oil change. Replace the oil filter and fill engine with normal quantity of fresh oil.

3. Remove battery and coat cable terminals with petroleum jelly. If there is evidence of acid spillage in the battery box, neutralize with baking soda, wash clean, and repaint the damaged area. Store the battery in a warm area and recharge it every 2 weeks.

4. Drain all gasoline from fuel tank, interconnecting hoses, and carburetors. Leave fuel petcock in the RESERVE position. As an alternative, a fuel preservative may be added to the fuel. This preservative is available from many motorcycle shops and marine equipment suppliers.

5. Remove spark plugs and add a small quantity of oil to each cylinder. Turn the engine a few revolutions by hand to distribute the oil and install the spark plugs.

6. Run a paper card, lightly saturated with silicone lubricant, between the points.

CAUTION
Do not use any other type of lubricant or the points will be burned when the bike is restored to service.

7. Check tire pressures. Move machine to storage area and store it on the centerstand.

2

CHAPTER THREE

TROUBLESHOOTING

Diagnosing mechanical problems is relatively simple if you use orderly procedures and keep a few basic principles in mind.

The troubleshooting procedures in this chapter analyze typical symptoms, and show logical methods of isolating causes. These are not the only methods. There may be several ways to solve a problem, but only a systematic approach can guarantee success.

Never assume anything. Do not overlook the obvious. If you are riding along and the bike suddenly quits, check the easiest, most accessible problem spots first. Is there gasoline in the tank? Is the gas petcock in the ON or RESERVE position? Has a spark plug wire fallen off? Check ignition switch. Sometimes the weight of keys on a key ring may turn the ignition off suddenly.

If nothing obvious turns up in a cursory check, look a little further. Learning to recognize and describe symptoms will make repairs easier for you or a mechanic at the shop. Describe problems accurately and fully. Saying that "it won't run" isn't the same as saying "it quit on the highway at high speed and wouldn't start," or that "it sat in my garage for 3 months and then wouldn't start."

Gather as many symptoms together as possible to aid in diagnosis. Note whether the engine lost power gradually or all at once, what color smoke (if any) came from the exhaust, and so on. Remember that the more complicated a machine is, the easier it is to troubleshoot because symptoms point to specific problems.

After the symptoms are defined, areas which could cause the problems are tested and analyzed. Guessing at the cause of a problem may provide the solution, but it can easily lead to frustration, wasted time, and a series of expensive, unnecessary parts replacement.

You do not need fancy equipment or complicated test gear to determine whether repairs can be attempted at home. A few simple checks could save a large repair bill and time lost while the bike sits in a dealer's service department. On the other hand, be realistic and do not attempt repairs beyond your abilities. Service departments tend to charge heavily for putting together a disassembled engine that may have been abused. Some won't even take on such a job — so use common sense, don't get in over your head.

OPERATING REQUIREMENTS

An engine needs 3 basics to run properly: correct gas/air mixture, compression, and a spark at the right time. If one or more are missing, the engine won't run. The electrical system is the weakest link of the 3 basics. More problems result from electrical breakdowns than from any other source. Keep that in mind before you begin tampering with carburetor adjustments and the like.

If a bike has been sitting for any length of time and refuses to start, check the battery for a charged condition first, and then look to the gasoline delivery system. This includes the tank, fuel pump, fuel petcock, lines, and the carburetors. Rust may have formed in the tank, obstructing fuel flow. Gasoline deposits may have gummed up carburetor jets and air passages. Gasoline tends to lose its potency after standing for long periods. Condensation may contaminate it with water. Drain old gas and try starting with a fresh tankful.

TROUBLESHOOTING INSTRUMENTS

Chapter One lists many of the instruments needed and detailed instructions on their use.

EMERGENCY TROUBLESHOOTING

When the bike is difficult to start or won't start at all, it does not help to grind away at the starter or kick the tires. Check for obvious problems even before getting out your tools. Go down the following list step-by-step. Do each one; you may be embarrassed to find your kill switch off, but that is better than wearing your battery down with the starter. If the bike still will not start, refer to the appropriate troubleshooting procedures which follow in this chapter.

1. Is there fuel in the tank? Remove the filler cap and rock the bike; listen for fuel sloshing around.

> **WARNING**
> *Do not use an open flame to check in the tank. A serious explosion is certain to result.*

2. Turn fuel petcock to RESERVE or PRIME to be sure that you get the last remaining gas.

3. Is the kill switch on?

4. Is the choke in the right position? It should be down for a cold engine and up for a warm engine.

5. Is the battery dead? Check it with a hydrometer.

6. Has the main fuse blown (**Figure 1**)? Replace it with a good one.

STARTER

Starter system troubles are relatively easy to isolate. The following are common symptoms and cures. **Figure 2** shows a wiring diagram of the starting system. Use it to help isolate troubles.

1. *Engine cranks very slowly or not at all* — If the headlight is very dim or not lighting at all, most likely the battery or its connecting wires are at fault. Check the battery using the procedures described in Chapter Seven. Check the wiring for breaks, shorts, and dirty connections.

If the battery and connecting wires check good, the trouble may be in the starter, solenoid, or wiring. To isolate the trouble, short the 2 large solenoid terminals together (not to ground); if the starter cranks normally, check the starter solenoid wiring. If the starter still fails to crank properly, remove the starter and test it.

2. *Starter engages but will not disengage when switch is released* — Usually caused by a faulty starter solenoid or switch.

CHARGING SYSTEM

Troubleshooting an alternator system is somewhat different from troubleshooting a generator system. For example, *never* short any terminals to ground on the alternator or voltage regulator.

The following symptoms are typical of alternator charging system troubles.

1. *Battery requires frequent charging* — The charging system is not functioning, or it is undercharging the battery. Test the alternator rectifier and voltage regulator as described in Chapter Seven.

2. *Battery requires frequent additions of water or lamps require frequent replacement* — The alternator is probably overcharging the battery. Have the voltage regulator checked or replaced.

3. *Noisy alternator* — Check for a loose alternator rotor bolt.

ENGINE

These procedures assume the starter cranks the engine normally. If not, refer to *Starter* in this chapter.

Poor Performance

1. *Engine misses erratically at all speeds* — Intermittent trouble like this can be difficult to find and correct. The fault could be in the ignition system, exhaust system (restriction), or fuel system. Follow troubleshooting procedures for these systems to isolate the trouble.

2. *Engine misses at idle only* — Trouble could exist anywhere in the ignition system. Follow

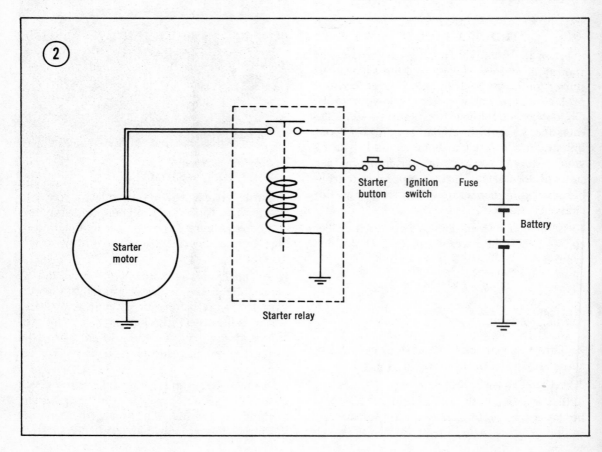

②

Starter motor

Starter button

Ignition switch

Fuse

Battery

Starter relay

the *ignition* troubleshooting procedure carefully. Trouble could exist in the carburetors' idle circuits. Check idle mixture adjustments (Chapter Two, *Carburetor Idle Adjustment*) and check for restrictions in the idle circuits.

3. *Engine misses at high speed only* — Trouble could exist in the fuel system or ignition system. Check the fuel lines and valve as described under *Fuel System* in this chapter. Also check spark plugs and high-tension leads (see *Ignition* in this chapter).

4. *Poor performance at all speeds, lack of acceleration* — Trouble usually exists in ignition or fuel system. Check each with the appropriate procedure. Also check for dragging brakes, tight or bound wheel bearings, and correct tire pressure.

5. *Excessive fuel consumption* — This can be caused by a wide variety of seemingly unrelated factors. Check for clutch slippage, dragging brakes, and defective wheel bearings. Check tire pressure. Check ignition and fuel systems.

ENGINE NOISES

1. *Valve clatter* — This is a light to heavy tapping sound from the cam box. It is usually caused by excessive valve clearance. Adjust the clearance as described in Chapter Four. If the noise persists, disassemble the valve drive system as described in Chapter Four and check for worn or damaged cam lobes, broken springs, missing adjustment shims, etc.

2. *Knocking or pinging during acceleration* — May be caused by lower octane fuel than recommended or by poor fuel available from some "discount" service stations. It may also be caused by incorrect ignition timing or spark plugs of wrong heat range. See Chapter Two, *Spark Plug Replacement* and *Ignition Timing*.

3. *Slapping or rattling noises at low speed or during acceleration* — May be caused by piston slap, i.e., excessive piston-to-cylinder wall clearance.

4. *Knocking or rapping during deceleration* — Usually caused by excessive rod bearing clearance.

5. *Persistent knocking and vibration* — Usually caused by excessive main bearing clearance.

6. *Rapid on-off squeal* — Compression leak around cylinder head gasket or spark plug.

EXCESSIVE VIBRATION

This can be difficult to locate without disassembling the engine. Usually this is caused by loose engine mounting hardware or worn engine and transmission bearings.

LUBRICATION TROUBLES

1. *Excessive oil consumption* — May be caused by worn rings and bores. Overhaul is necessary to correct this. See Chapter Four. It may also be caused by worn valve guides or defective valve guide seals. Also check for exterior leaks.

2. *Oil pressure lamp does not light when ignition switch is on* — Locate the oil pressure sender on right side of engine. See **Figure 3**. Ensure that the wire is connected to the sender and makes good contact. Pull off wire and ground it. If the lamp lights, replace the sender. If the lamp does not light, replace the lamp.

3. Oil pressure lamp lights or flickers when engine is running — This indicates low or complete loss of oil pressure. *Stop the engine immediately;* coast to a stop with the clutch disengaged. This may simply be caused by a low oil level; check the oil level. Check for a shorted oil pressure sender with an ohmmeter or other continuity tester. Listen for unusual noises indicating bad bearings, etc. Do not restart the engine until you know why the light went on and the problem has been corrected.

FUEL SYSTEM

Fuel system trouble must be isolated to the carburetor or fuel lines. These procedures assume that the ignition system has been checked and correctly adjusted.

1. *Engine will not start* — First determine that fuel is being delivered to the carburetors. Disconnect the fuel line at the carburetor. Insert the end of the line in a small container to catch the fuel. Turn the tap to RUN. Fuel should run from the line. If not, remove the tap from the tank and clean and check it. See Chapter Six.

2. *Rough idle or engine misses and stalls frequently* — Check carburetor adjustments. See Chapter Two.

3. *Stumbling when starting from idle* — Check idle speed adjustment. See Chapter Two.

4. *Engine misses at high speed or lacks power* — Possible fuel starvation. Check fuel delivery. Clean main jets and float needle valves.

5. *Black exhaust smoke* — Black exhaust smoke indicates a badly overrich mixture. Make sure the chokes disengage. Check idle mixture and idle speed. Check for leaky float needle valves and correct float level. Make sure jets are correct size. See Chapter Six.

CLUTCH

All clutch work except adjustment requires removal of the right rear engine cover. See Chapter Five.

1. *Slippage* — This is most noticeable when accelerating in a high gear from low speed. To check slippage, start the engine, select 2nd gear, and release the clutch as if riding off in 1st gear. If the clutch is good, the engine will slow and stall. If the clutch slips, increased engine speed will be apparent.

Slippage results from insufficient clutch lever free play, worn plates, or weak springs.

2. *Drag or failure to release* — This usually causes difficult shifting and gear clash, particularly when downshifting. The cause may be excessive clutch lever free play, warped or bent plates, broken or loose lining, or lack of lubrication in clutch actuating mechanism.

3. *Chatter or grabbing* — Check for worn or warped plates. Check clutch lever free play.

TRANSMISSION

Transmission problems are usually indicated by one or more of the following symptoms:

   a. Difficulty shifting gears

   b. Gear clash when downshifting

   c. Slipping out of gear

   d. Excessive noise in neutral

   e. Excessive noise in gear

Transmission symptoms are sometimes hard to distinguish from clutch symptoms. Be sure that the clutch is not causing the trouble before working on the transmission.

BRAKES

1. *Brake lever or pedal goes all the way to its stop* — There are numerous causes for this including excessively worn pads, air in the hydraulic system, leaky brake lines, leaky calipers, or leaky or worn master cylinder. Check for leaks and thin brake pads. Bleed the brakes. If this does not cure the trouble, rebuild the calipers and/or master cylinder.

2. *Spongy lever or pedal* — Normally caused by air in the system; bleed the brakes.

3. *Dragging brakes* — Check for swollen rubber parts due to improper brake fluid or contamination, and obstructed master cylinder bypass port. Clean or replace defective parts.

4. *Hard lever or pedal* — Check brake pads for contamination. Also check for restricted brake lines and hoses.

5. *High speed fade* — Check for contaminated brake pads. Ensure that recommended brake fluid is installed. Drain entire system and refill if in doubt.

6. *Pulsating lever or pedal* — Check for excessive brake disc runout. Undetected accident damage is also a frequent cause of this.

LIGHTING SYSTEM

Bulbs which continuously burn out may be caused by excessive vibration, loose connections that permit sudden current surges, poor battery connections, or installation of the wrong type bulb.

A majority of light and horn or other electrical accessory problems are caused by loose or corroded ground connections. Check those first, and then substitute known good units for easier troubleshooting.

FRONT SUSPENSION AND STEERING

1. *Too stiff or too soft* — Make sure forks have not been leaking and oil is correct viscosity. If in doubt, drain and refill as described in Chapter Two.

2. *Leakage around seals* — There should be a light film of oil on fork tubes. However, large amounts of oil on tubes means the seals are leaking. Replace seals. See Chapter Nine.

3. *Fork action is rough* — Check for bent tube.

4. *Steering wobbles* — Check for correct steering head bearing tightness. See Chapter Nine.

3

CHAPTER FOUR

ENGINE

The GS750 engine is an air-cooled, transversely mounted, in-line four with DOHC. Five main bearings support the crankshaft in a horizontally split crankcase. The crankshaft assembly is pressed together. One-piece rods are carried on roller bearings on the big end. The camshafts are driven through a chain, from the crankshaft. Tension is controlled by a spring-loaded slipper tensioner bearing against the rear vertical run of the chain. Primary drive is by gear. The ignition contact breaker is driven from the right end of the crankshaft.

Lubrication system is a wet-sump type. The engine and transmission share a common oil supply. The clutch is a wet type, located outboard of the transmission case, inside the right engine cover.

This chapter provides complete service and overhaul procedures for the GS750 engine. Specifications and wear limits are summarized in **Table 1,** which appears at the end of the chapter. **Table 2**, also located at the end of the chapter, summarizes critical torque for engine fasteners.

Although the clutch and transmission are integral with the engine, they are covered separately in Chapter Five to simplify the procedures.

ENGINE REMOVAL/INSTALLATION

The engine can be removed in several states of disassembly. Most commonly it would be removed with the upper end intact, such as during frame repair or painting or transmission service; or it would be removed extensively disassembled, such as during a major overhaul.

The procedure presented here is the more detailed task, involving much disassembly of the engine while it is still in the motorcycle. The motorcycle makes an excellent engine jig and parts such as the clutch, cylinder head, cylinder block, etc., are more easily removed than if the engine were on a bench.

For the shortened procedure which maintains the engine essentially intact, perform Steps 1 through 13, 26 through 30, and 37 through 40.

1. Set the motorcycle on the centerstand. Remove accessories such as fairing and crash bars.

2. Drain the engine oil. Don't forget to remove the filter housing cover and allow the filter cavity to drain as well; it holds considerable oil and could create a mess on the workbench after the engine has been removed.

3. Raise the seat and disconnect the battery leads — negative first, then positive. This is a

good time to remove the battery, service it and charge it as described in Chapter Seven.

4. Turn the fuel tank petcock to FUEL, not to PRIME, and disconnect the lines. There is no need to drain the fuel. Unscrew the rear fuel tank mounting bolt (**Figure 1**). Pull the tank back and off the front rubber mounting pads.

> NOTE: *Before installing the tank, lubricate the mounting pads with rubber lube or WD-40 to make installation and later removal easier.*

5. Unscrew the flange mounting nuts from the exhaust head pipes (**Figure 2**) and loosen the pinch bolts that hold the head pipes in the mufflers. Pull the headpipes out of the mufflers, then remove the mufflers.

> NOTE: *The mufflers can be left in place on the motorcycle; however, work may be a little easier if they are removed.*

6. Remove the air cleaner cover (**Figure 3**) and the air cleaner element (**Figure 4**).

7. Disconnect the breather hose that connects the camshaft cover to the air cleaner box (**Figure 5**).

8. Loosen the clamps on the hoses that connect the carburetors to the air cleaner box (**Figure 6**).

4

9. Remove the bolts that attach the air cleaner box to the frame (**Figure 7**). Disconnect the hoses and remove the air cleaner box from the motorcycle.

10. Disconnect the green/yellow lead from the main electrical harness (**Figure 8**). This is the oil pressure sender lead.

11. Loosen the locknuts on the throttle cable adjusters (**Figure 9**), screw the adjusters in to release tension from the cables and disconnect the cables from the quadrant.

12. Loosen the hose clamps that mount the carburetors on the engine (**Figure 10**). Pull rearward on the carburetors to disconnect them from the engine and remove them from the motorcycle as an assembly.

13. Disconnect the high-tension leads from the spark plugs by grasping the caps, not the wires. Unscrew the spark plugs from the cylinder head and mark them for location so that they may be later inspected and any abnormal conditions isolated to a particular cylinder. Disconnect the high-tension leads from the clips.

> NOTE: *Before proceeding with engine removal, carry out a compression check to be used as a guide for required work. Compression testing is described in detail in Chapter Two. The compression readings for the engine shown were: No. 4 (right side), 135 psi; No. 3, 130 psi; No. 2, 125 psi; No. 1, 115 psi. The standard compression range is 128-171 psi (9-12 kg^2); however, the service limit is 100 psi (7 kg^2), indicating that the cylinder conditions in this case are acceptable.*

14. Unscrew the bolts that attach the camshaft breather cover (**Figure 11**), remove the breather and collect the gauze strainers.

15. Remove the end caps from the camshaft boxes (**Figure 12**). Unscrew the 16 bolts that hold the camshaft cover in place. Note the location of the high-tension spark plug lead clips (**Figure 13**) on the outboard rear bolts. Tap the cover around the sealing surface with a soft mallet to break it loose and remove the cover.

NOTE: *Before removing the camshafts, check each of the valve tappet clearances with a flat feeler gauge and record the readings, by valve and by cylinder, for reference during reassembly. Any out-of-specification clearances must be corrected, as described in Chapter Two under* **Engine Tune-Up**.

16. Loosen the locknut on the cam chain tensioner and run in the center screw to lock the tensioner in place and prevent it from releasing when it is removed from the engine (**Figure 14**). Unscrew the 3 bolts that mount the tensioner to the engine and remove the tensioner.

17. Note the marks — A, B, C, and D — on the cam bearing caps and the corresponding marks in the cam box (**Figure 15**). The cam bearing caps must be installed in the respective locations when the head is reassembled. Note also the marks on the camshafts indicating intake and exhaust, and right and left. It is essential that they be reinstalled in the positions and orientation from which they were removed. Otherwise, severe engine damage will result.

18. Loosen the bolts in the cam bearing caps in a crisscross pattern, progressively from cap to cap, until valve spring tension has been relieved. Then unscrew the bolts and remove the caps.

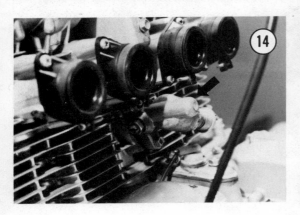

19. Unscrew the bolts from the upper cam chain idler (**Figure 16**) and remove it. Take care to collect the resilient mounting blocks and spacer, noting their locations for reference during assembly.

20. Before removing the camshafts, wire the cam chain to the frame so it will not drop into the engine. Pry the speedometer drive out of the cambox (**Figure 17**). Take care not to drop the drive gear.

21. Unscrew the cylinder head nuts in the pattern shown in **Figure 18**. Don't overlook the 10mm bolts at each end of the cylinder head.

22. Pull the front rubber chain guide out of the cylinder head (**Figure 19**). Tap around the base of the cylinder head with a soft mallet, and with assistance lift the head and remove it from the engine.

CAUTION
Do not invert the head to remove washers and nuts; the valve tappets and clearance adjustment shims will very likely fall out as well. This will require a time-consuming job of measuring valve clearance once again so the shims can be returned to their respective tappets, and it may be unnecessary if the clearances were within specification. Use a magnet to retrieve the washers and nuts.

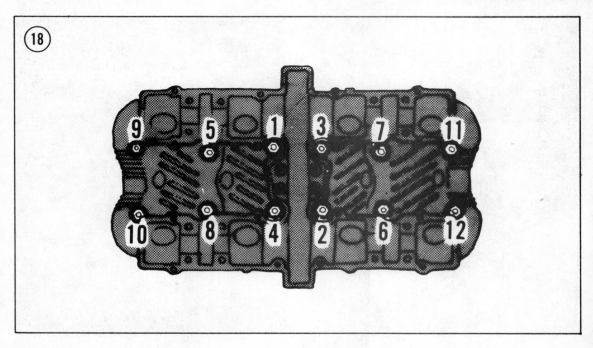

23. Remove the cylinder head gasket and note the marking TOP. This mark must face up when the gasket is installed.

24. Remove the rectangular rubber seal from the groove in the top of the cylinder block.

25. With assistance, carefully lift the cylinder block, taking care not to let the pistons fall against the crankcase. When the cylinder block has been removed, place piston blocks beneath the two center pistons and carefully rotate the crankshaft to bring the pistons down onto the blocks (**Figure 20**).

26. On the left side of the motorcycle, loosen the rear footpeg mounting bolt, unscrew the front bolt, and swing the peg down. Unscrew the bolt from the gear selector lever and remove the lever (**Figure 21**). The bolt must be removed, not just loosened; there is a groove cut into the shaft that is engaged by the bolt.

27. Remove the clutch adjuster cover (**Figure 22**). Unscrew the 2 screws inside the adjuster cavity and the 4 screws around the outside of the cover (**Figure 23**). Remove the cover and swing it out of the way.

4

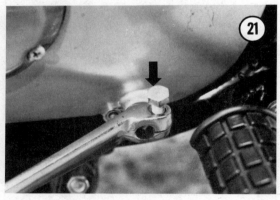

28. Loosen the clutch adjuster locknut and loosen the adjuster to remove tension from the cable (**Figure 24**). Straighten the tab inside the clevis that locks the cable into the clevis, and disconnect the cable (**Figure 25**). Unscrew the adjuster from the cover, pull out the cable, and set the cover aside.

29. Loosen the screws in the left engine cover with an impact driver, then unscrew them (**Figure 26**). Tap lightly around the edge of the cover to break it loose. Remove the cover. Pull the alternator wiring harness out of the case. Collect the shim from the end of the starter idler gearshaft (**Figure 27**).

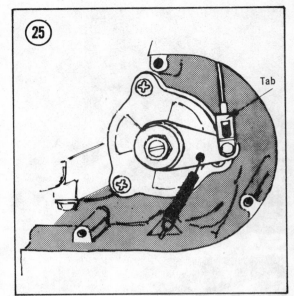

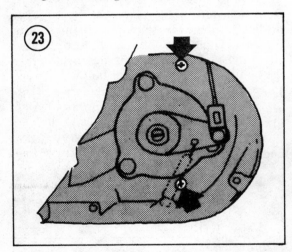

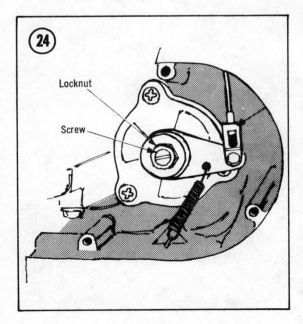

30. Remove the bolt from the kickstarter lever (**Figure 28**) and pull the kickstarter lever off the shaft. Like the gear selector lever, the bolt must be completely removed.

31. Loosen the screws in the clutch-side cover with an impact driver, unscrew them, and remove the cover (**Figure 29**).

32. Temporarily install the gear selector lever and shift the transmission into 1st gear. Apply the rear brake and loosen the clutch bolts in a crisscross pattern (**Figure 30**). Also refer to **Figure 31**. Unscrew the bolts, remove the

4

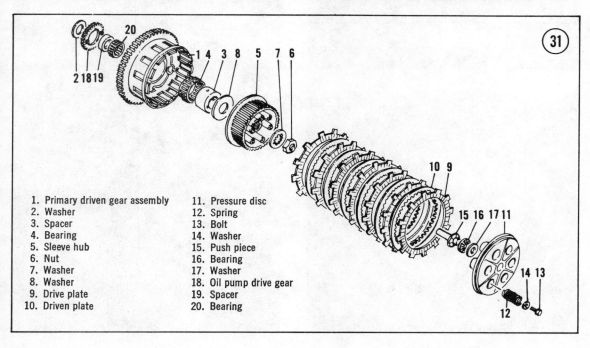

1. Primary driven gear assembly
2. Washer
3. Spacer
4. Bearing
5. Sleeve hub
6. Nut
7. Washer
8. Washer
9. Drive plate
10. Driven plate
11. Pressure disc
12. Spring
13. Bolt
14. Washer
15. Push piece
16. Bearing
17. Washer
18. Oil pump drive gear
19. Spacer
20. Bearing

springs and outer pressure plate (**Figure 32**), and the clutch plates (**Figure 33**).

33. Straighten the tab washer on the clutch hub nut and unscrew the nut with an impact driver (**Figure 34**). This can be done without the use of a special clutch holding tool; wrap the inner clutch basket with a shop rag, have someone hold it, and loosen the nut with the driver. Remove the tab washer, the hub, and the thrust washer behind the hub. Notice the grooves in the thrust washer face (**Figure 35**). These must face in when the washer is installed.

34. Install one or two 6mm screws into spacer (3, **Figure 31**). Pull out on screws and remove spacer, then bearing, **Figure 36**. Shift clutch basket toward rear of engine until primary gear on clutch assembly clears crankcase and lift out clutch assembly. Remove oil pump drive gear, bearing, spacer and washer.

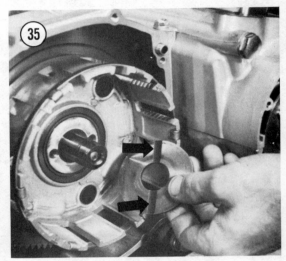

35. With an impact driver, loosen the screws in the bearing and seal retainers on the right side (**Figure 37**), and in the seal retainer on the left side (**Figure 38**).

36. Straighten the tab washer on the countershaft sprocket nut and loosen the nut with an impact driver. Use the rear brake to prevent the sprocket from rotating. Remove the sprocket and collect the spacer located behind it (**Figure 39**). Remove the ignition.

37. Unscrew the nuts from the right and left ends of the front and rear engine mount cross bolts (**Figure 40**). Remove the bolts. Unscrew the bolts from the front engine mount tabs and remove them from the frame. Unscrew the right and left bottom engine mounting bolts (**Figure 41**). Note that they are held with blind nuts and fitted with spacers.

4

38. Double check to make sure all electrical connections between the engine and the chassis have been parted. Check also for breather hoses and tubes and disconnect any that may have been overlooked. Then, with assistance, remove the engine from the right side of motorcycle.

39. To install the engine, follow the removal steps exactly in reverse order. Refer to **Table 2** at the end of the chapter for all critical torques. Refer to *Cylinder Head Service — Installation* and time the camshafts with the crankshaft. Refer to *Cylinder Head Service* and tighten the nuts and bolts in the pattern shown to the torques specified. When installation is complete, refer to Chapter Two and service and tune the engine.

BOTTOM END
DISASSEMBLY/ASSEMBLY

Before removing the crankcase bolts, make a cardboard template following the pattern shown in **Figure 42**. Punch holes in each of the bolt locations. As each bolt is removed, place it in the template in the corresponding location. This will greatly speed up assembly time by eliminating the search for the correct bolt for each hole.

1. Remove the seal and bearing retainers from the right (**Figure 43**) and left sides (**Figure 44**) of the engine. These are the ones whose screws were loosened before the engine was removed from the motorcycle.

2. Remove the idler gear from the right side.

3. Collect the O-rings from the pump bores between the crankcase and the transmission.

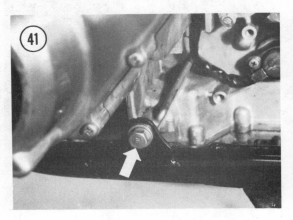

4. Double nut the upper stud on the oil filter cavity (**Figure 45**) and unscrew it to gain access to the crankcase bolt above it.

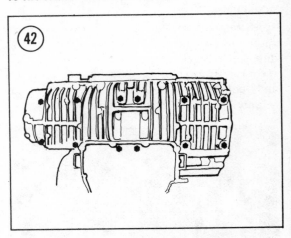

5. Unscrew the crankcase bolts and arrange them in the template as described above.

6. With the engine inverted, tap around the sealing surface of the case halves to break them

loose. Then, lift the lower crankcase half off the upper half. The transmission will remain in the upper case half.

7. Refer to Chapter Five and remove the transmission gearsets and shifting mechanism.

8. With assistance, remove the piston blocks and lift straight up on the crankshaft assembly to remove it from the upper case half.

9. Follow the disassembly steps in reverse to assemble the bottom end. Before proceeding, however, refer to *Bottom End Inspection*, this chapter, and the transmission inspection procedures in Chapter Five.

10. When installing the crankshaft in the upper case half, make sure the half-ring that locates the crankshaft laterally is installed in its groove (**Figure 46**). The ring must fit into the groove in the right-end bearing (**Figure 47**). Also, the other bearings must engage the pins in the bearing bores (**Figure 48**).

11. Position the right-end seal with the grooved face facing out (**Figure 49**).

12. Coat the sealing surface of the upper case half with gasket cement. If the alignment dowels were removed, install them. Apply a light coat of gasket cement to the sealing surface of the bottom case half.

13. Squirt oil into the main bearings, the connecting rod big end bearings, the transmission bearings, and over the transmission gears. Slowly rotate the transmission gears to distribute the oil. This step is essential to ensure that lubrication will be provided when the engine is first started, before the pump begins to provide lubrication.

14. With the crankshaft and transmission installed, set the bottom case half in place and press it down firmly and evenly by hand until the sealing surfaces contact. It may be necessary to tap lightly with a soft mallet, particularly in the areas of the alignment dowels. However, the case halves should meet all along their sealing surfaces before the bolts are installed. Do not use the bolts to pull the cases together; if they do not meet, remove the bottom case half and check for the reason for the resistance.

15. Remove one bolt at a time from the template and start it into its respective hole — just a few turns until all the bolts are in place. Then run them in as shown in the pattern (**Figure 50**) just until they make contact with the case. Don't tighten them yet.

16. Invert the engine and install the upper case bolts in the same manner as for the bottom case bolts. (**Figure 51**).

17. Turn the engine upside down once again and tighten the bolts in the pattern shown (**Figure 50**). The specified torque for the 6mm bolts is 1 mkg (7.2 ft.-lb.); for the 8mm bolts the torque is 2 mkg (14.5 ft.-lb.). Invert the engine and tighten the upper bolts in the pattern shown (**Figure 51**) to the same torque values.

18. Install the sump cover and tighten the bolts in a crisscross pattern to 1 mkg (7.2 ft.-lb.).

19. Apply liquid locking compound to the threads of the seal and bearing retainer screws and install the retainers.

20. The remaining assembly steps can be carried out after the engine is installed in the motorcycle.

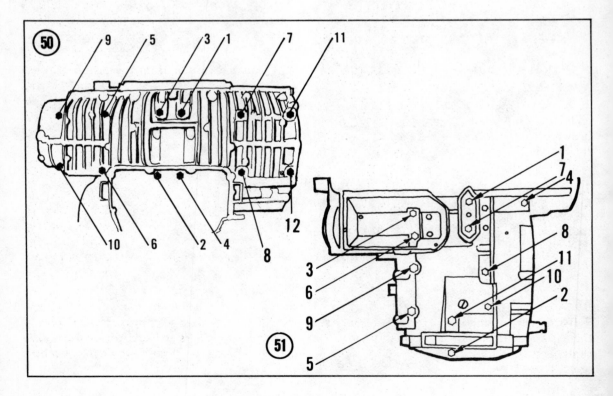

BOTTOM END INSPECTION

With the exception of seal replacement and some preliminary checks, crankshaft service should be entrusted to a dealer. The crankshaft is pressed together and requires a press to separate and assemble it, as well as considerable experience to ensure that it is correctly aligned. In most cases where crankcase service is required, it is likely that the entire assembly will be replaced with a factory-assembled unit. Be consoled, however, that crankshaft service is not likely to be required throughout the life of the motorcycle unless it is damaged by loss of oil or a piston failure — also unlikely.

1. Check the crankshaft outboard of the seals for signs of excessive oil (**Figure 52**). The crankshaft should be almost dry in these areas at the time of disassembly. If it is not, remove the seals and check for gouges or other damage. If damage or wear are apparent, replace the seals.

2. Inspect the connecting rod big and small ends for heat damage, indicated by a deep brown color in the area of the bearing bores. If this condition exists, refer the assembly to a dealer for further checking.

3. In turn, grasp each of the connecting rods, pull up on it, and rap it with the heel of your other hand. Listen for the sharp metallic click that indicates wear.

> NOTE: *To check the rods in this manner it is first necessary to remove the pistons. See Cylinder Head Service in this chapter.*

If after performing the checks just mentioned there is doubt about the condition of the crankshaft, entrust it to a dealer for precise inspection.

CYLINDER HEAD SERVICE

Cylinder head service can range from a simple decarbonizing all the way to valve and guide replacement. Major work such as valve seat reconditioning and valve guide replacement should be entrusted to a dealer or a competent motorcycle or automotive rebuilding service.

Cylinder Head Removal

Refer to *Engine Removal/Installation* at the beginning of this chapter and carry out Steps 1 through 22 to remove the cylinder head from the engine; the engine can remain in the motorcycle.

Cylinder Head Inspection

1. Remove all traces of gasket from the head and from the sealing surface of the cylinder block.

2. Without removing the valves, remove all of the carbon deposits from the combustion chambers with a wire brush and solvent. Stubborn deposits can be removed with a blunt scraper made of soft aluminum or hardwood. Steel scrapers and screwdrivers tend to damage the combustion chamber surfaces.

3. After all the carbon has been removed from the combustion chambers and exhaust ports, clean the entire head in solvent.

4. Clean the carbon from the piston crowns. Do not remove the carbon ridges from the tops of the cylinders; if the ridges are removed, excessive oil consumption is likely to occur.

5. Check the combustion chambers and ports for cracks. While it is possible to repair such damage with heliarc welding, the services of someone qualified to do the job are usually very costly. In addition, the cylinder head would then require machining of the sealing surface to true it. This, in turn, could require that the combustion chambers be domed to restore the compression ratio to specifications. For ·these reasons, it is best to replace a cracked cylinder head with a new one.

6. Push the valve stems sideways with your thumb and check for apparent play. If play is evident, the guides are probably worn and should be replaced. See *Valve Guide Replacement*.

4

Installation

1. Install a new cylinder head gasket on the cylinder block. The word TOP must face up **(Figure 53)**. Install rectangular rubber seal in groove. Rotate the crankshaft to align the T mark for No. 1 and 4 cylinders with the stationary timing mark **(Figure 54)**.

2. Set the cylinder head on the studs and with assistance, hold it up until the camshaft drive chain has been fed up through the gallery in the head **(Figure 55)**.

3. Slowly slide the head down and into position. Make sure the alignment dowels are engaged before pressing it all the way down.

4. Install the 4 cap nuts with copper washers **(Figure 56)**. Install the 8 plain nuts with washers and tighten them in the sequence shown to 3.5-4.0 mkg (25-29 ft.-lb.).

5. Install the two 6mm bolts **(Figure 57)** and tighten them to 0.7-1.1 mkg (5-8 ft.-lb.).

6. Install the valve tappets and shims after oiling them with fresh engine oil.

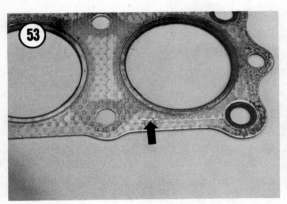

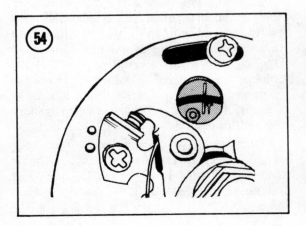

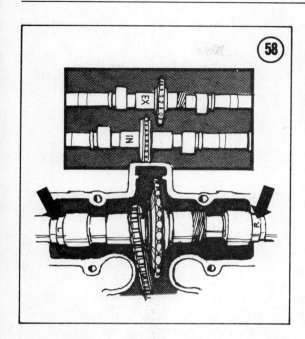

7. Set the exhaust camshaft (stamped EX) in the forward cam-bed with the R mark to the right and the L mark to the left (**Figure 58**). Don't forget to pass the camshaft through the chain.

8. Set the intake camshaft (stamped IN) in the rear cam-bed with the R mark to the right and the L mark to the left.

> NOTE: *Prior to setting the camshafts in place, coat the camshaft journals thoroughly with molybdenum disulphide; the coating must be complete, without voids. Then oil the journal bearings with fresh engine oil.*

9. Check to make sure the crankshaft has not moved; the T 1-4 mark on the advance plate must line up with the stationary timing mark. Then pull up on the front run of the chain to remove all slack. Position the exhaust camshaft so the "1" mark aligns with the sealing surface of the cam box (**Figure 59**) and engage it with the chain. Don't allow any slack in the chain. The "2" mark should point straight up.

10. Count 20 pins from the "2" mark on the exhaust camshaft sprocket toward the intake camshaft (**Figure 60**). Engage the 20th pin with the intake sprocket above the "3" mark on the intake camshaft sprocket. This is the basic camshaft/crankshaft timing. Don't allow the chain to become disengaged.

11. Set the camshaft bearing caps in place, matching their letters with the letters in the cylinder head (**Figure 61**). Screw the cap bolts in finger-tight. Check to see that the relationship of the camshafts and the crankshaft have not changed.

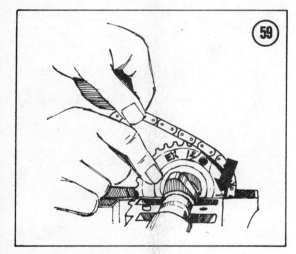

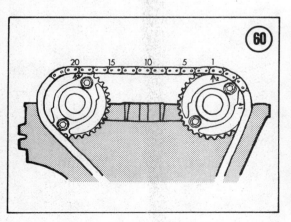

12. Progressively tighten the camshaft bearing cap bolts in a crisscross pattern **(Figure 62)**, back and forth from one cap to the other until the camshafts are pulled evenly down into their bearings. Then tighten them, in a crisscross pattern, to 0.4-0.6 mkg (2.9-4.3 ft.-lb.). Once again, check to see that the camshaft timing has not changed.

> CAUTION
> *When camshafts are properly torqued, No. 1 mark on exhaust cam must point **exactly** toward or **slightly below** (1-2mm) gasket surface, (Figure 59). If mark is even slightly above gasket surface, timing is retarded and must be corrected. Repeat camshaft timing procedure and advance both camshafts the necessary amount (usually 1 tooth) until correct timing is achieved.*

13. Install the top camshaft chain idler assembly **(Figure 63)**. The camshafts will rotate slightly as the idler is cinched down, but this is all right provided the relationship of the crankshaft and camshaft sprockets remains the same as described in Steps 8 and 9.

14. Install the front camshaft chain guide **(Figure 64)**. The ears on the top of the guide must engage the recesses in the cambox.

15. Refer to Chapter Two, *Valve Clearance Measurement* and *Adjusting Valve Clearance,* and check the clearance and adjust it if necessary.

16. Assemble the valve chain tensioner **(Figure 65)**. Wind the knurled tensioner knob counterclockwise and at the same time push the tensioner rod into the tensioner body. Lock it in place with the lockscrew. Install the tensioner on the rear of the cylinder block **(Figure 66)**.

17. Loosen the lockscrew ¼ turn to allow the tensioner rod to come into contact with the chain tensioner slipper. Then tighten the locknut on the lockscrew **(Figure 67)**.

18. Check the operation of the tensioner by rotating the crankshaft and the tensioner knob counterclockwise. This allows the chain to push the tensioner rod back into the tensioner. Then rotate the crankshaft clockwise and watch the tensioner knob. It should also rotate clockwise **(Figure 68)** as spring pressure moves the ten-

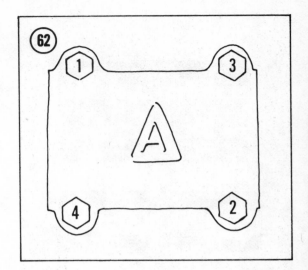

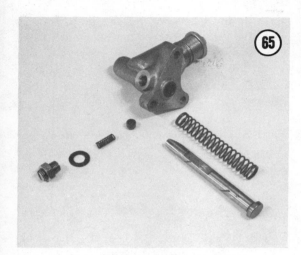

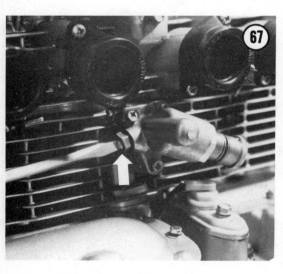

sioner rod forward to remove the slack from the chain.

19. Continue assembly as described under *Engine Removal/Installation* in this chapter.

VALVES AND VALVE SEATS

Removal

Refer to **Figure 69** for this procedure.

1. Remove the cylinder head as described under *Cylinder Head Removal*. Remove the tappets from the tappet bores.

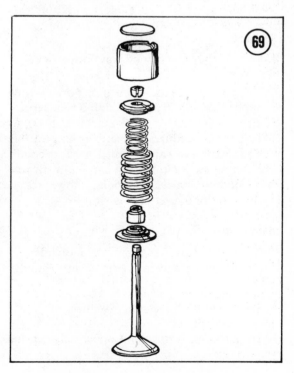

2. Compress the valve springs with a valve spring compressor, remove the valve keepers, and release the tension on the compressor. Do this for each of the valves.

3. Remove the valve spring caps, springs, and valves. Identify each part for location.

Inspection

1. Clean the valves with a wire brush and solvent. Discard any valves that are burned, warped, or cracked. Salvageable valves should be entrusted to a dealer or automotive machine shop for grinding.

2. With a micrometer, measure the valve stems for wear. Compare the actual measurements with the specifications in **Table 1** (at the end of the chapter).

3. Remove all carbon and varnish from the valve guides with a stiff spiral wire brush.

4. Insert each valve in its guide. Hold the valve just slightly off its seats and rock it sideways. If it rocks more than slightly, the guide is probably worn and should be replaced. As a final check, take head to a dealer and have the valve guides measured.

5. Measure the valve spring heights. All should be of length specified in **Table 1** with no bends or other distortion. Replace defective springs.

6. Check the valve spring retainer and valve keepers. If they are in good condition, they may be reused.

7. Inspect valve seats. If worn or burned, they must be reconditioned. This should be performed by your dealer or local machine shop, although the procedure is described later in this section. Seats and valves in near-perfect condition can be reconditioned by lapping with fine carborundum paste. Lapping, however, is always inferior to precision grinding.

Installation

1. Coat the valve stems with molybdenum disulphide paste and insert them into cylinder head.

2. Install bottom spring retainers and new seals. See **Figure 69**.

3. Install valve springs and upper valve spring retainers.

4. Push down on upper valve spring retainers with the valve spring compressor and install valve keepers (**Figure 70**).

5. With a soft drift and hammer, rap sharply on each valve stem to seat the valve keepers (**Figure 71**).

Valve Guide Replacement

When guides are worn so that there is excessive stem-to-guide clearance or valve tipping, they must be replaced. Replace all, even if

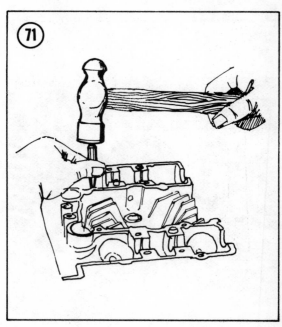

only one is worn. This job should only be done by a dealer as special tools are required.

Valve Seat Reconditioning

This job is best left to your dealer or local machine shop. They have the special equipment and knowledge for this exacting job. You can still save considerable money by removing the cylinder head and taking just the head to the shop. The following procedure is provided in the event that you are not near a dealer and the local machine shop is not familiar with the GS750.

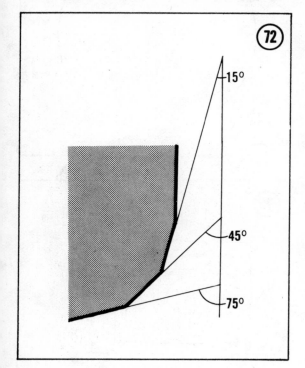

1. With a 15° valve seat cutter, remove just enough metal to make the bottom of the seat concentric. See **Figure 72**.

2. With a 75° valve seat cutter, remove just enough metal from the top of the seat to make it concentric.

3. With a 45° valve seat cutter, cut a seat that is 1.0-1.2mm (0.039-0.047 in.) wide.

4. Coat the valve face with Prussian blue.

5. Insert the valve into the guide.

6. With light pressure, rotate the valve ¼ turn.

7. Lift out the valve. If the valve seats properly, the blue dye will transfer evenly to the valve seat face. If it does not, carefully hand lap the valve to the seat, using a fine grade lapping compound until the valve-to-seat contact is complete.

PISTON/CYLINDER SERVICE

Piston and cylinder work can be carried out with the engine in the motorcycle. Refer to *Engine Removal/Installation* at the beginning of this chapter and perform Steps 1 through 25. Then proceed as described below.

1. Cover the crankcase openings with clean shop rags to prevent dirt, moisture and snap rings from entering the engine.

2. Remove the snap rings from the No. 1 piston **(Figure 73)**.

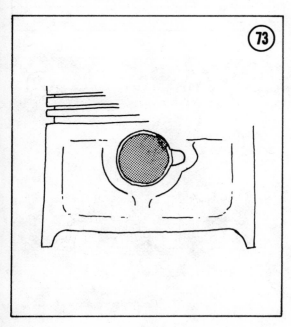

3. Press the pin out of the rod and piston and remove the piston. With an indelible marking pen, write the cylinder number on the inside of the piston — in this case, "1".

4. Place the pin in the inverted piston. It is essential that the parts remain in sets and are not mixed with other parts. Discard snap rings.

5. Remove the other pistons in the manner just described.

Inspection

1. With an inside micrometer or cylinder gauge, measure each of the cylinder bores at 3 locations (**Figure 74** and in 2 planes, 90° apart (**Figure 75**). Compare the actual dimensions to **Table 1** and rebore the cylinders if any of the measurements exceed the service limit.

The cylinders should be rebored also if the surface is scored or abraded. Pistons are available in oversize increases of 0.5mm (0.0197 in.) and 1.0mm (0.0394 in.). Purchase the pistons before the cylinders are bored so that the pistons can be measured and the cylinders bored accordingly to maintain correct piston-to-cylinder clearance.

2. With a micrometer, measure the pistons at the points shown in **Figure 76**. Refer to **Table 1**. If any piston is less than the service limit at any one point, they should be replaced as a set. It may not be necessary to install oversize pistons if the cylinder bores are good and within service limits (see Step 1 above). If the pistons are within the service limit, proceed with the next steps.

3. Clean the piston crown with a soft metal scraper to remove carbon. Use a piece of old piston ring to clean ring grooves (**Figure 77**).

4. With a flat feeler gauge, check the side clearance of the rings in the grooves (**Figure 78**). If the clearance is greater than that shown in **Table 1**, measure the ring thickness, then the groove width to determine which is

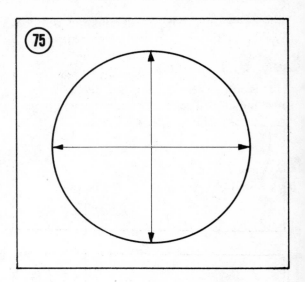

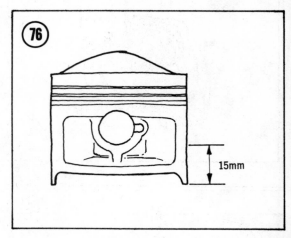

15mm

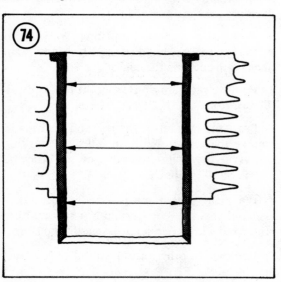

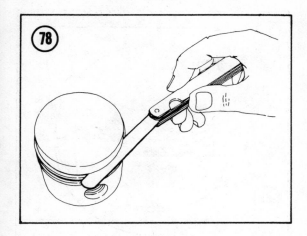

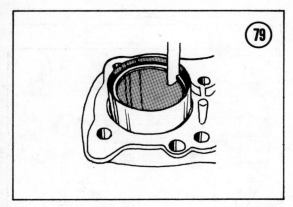

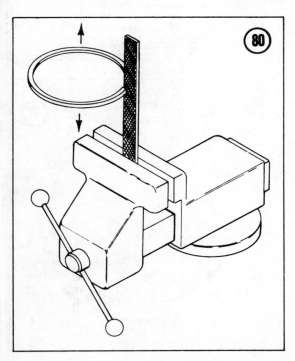

worn. All pieces that are worn beyond their respective service should be replaced. Ring thickness and groove width standards and service limits are also shown in **Table 1**.

5. Place the 2 top piston rings, one at a time, into the cylinder bore and measure the end gap (**Figure 79**). This is required for new rings as well as old ones. Compare the actual gap to **Table 1** and replace old rings if their gap is greater than the service limit. For new rings, it is more likely that the gap will be less minimum standard. If such is the case, clamp a fine, small file in a vise and file the ring ends as shown in **Figure 80**.

6. Measure the free-state ring gap with a caliper as shown in **Figure 81**. If the in-cylinder gap is correct, but the free-state gap is less than the service limit (**Table 1**), the ring will not seal well and should be replaced.

> NOTE: *The inspection steps above are designed to determine overall condition of the upper end; they should not be used to isolate one or two out-of-spec parts, such as one piston or a couple of rings. While some of the parts may be within service limits it is best that all like parts be replaced at the same time as long as the out-of-spec condition is caused by normal wear.*

4

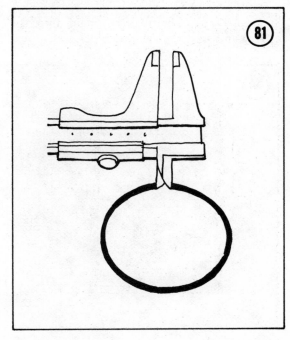

Assembly

1. Assemble the upper end by reversing the disassembly steps.

2. Lightly oil the cylinder bores before installing the cylinder block.

3. Oil the connecting rod small ends. Use new snap rings and install the pistons on their respective rods with the stamped arrow on the crown pointing forward (**Figure 82**).

4. Identify piston rings in each set and install them in the appropriate groove (**Figure 83**).

The top ring is plated and appears shinier than the 2nd ring. Install the rings with the marked side up. Install the oil ring spacer and check to see if its end overlap or abut (**Figure 84**). If they do, file the ends carefully to provide some clearance.

5. Stagger the ring gaps as shown in **Figure 85**.

6. Before installing the cylinder block, check to make sure that the large O-rings are fitted to each of the cylinder spigots (**Figure 86**) and that they are in good condition. Replace any that are not.

7. Place the piston blocks under pistons No. 2 and No. 3. Install ring compressors on pistons No. 2 and 3. If you do not have ring compressors, hose clamps will work as well — and they are a lot less money than piston ring compressors (**Figure 87**).

8. Feed the camshaft drive chain into the gallery and start the cylinder block down over

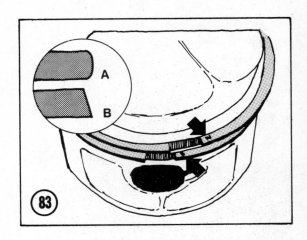

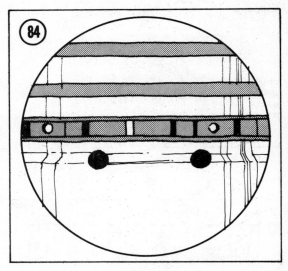

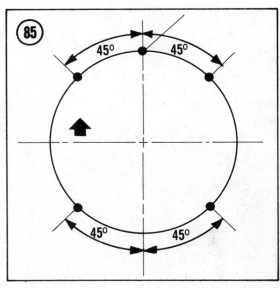

the studs. Press it down over the pistons until the compressors have been pushed free of the rings. Then remove the compressors.

9. Rotate the crankshaft slowly clockwise, taking care not to pull the No. 2 and 3 pistons out of the cylinders. Install the compressors on the No. 1 and 4 pistons. Hold the crankshaft to

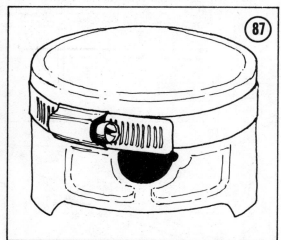

prevent it from turning, and push the cylinder block down until the compressors have been displaced from the rings. Then remove the compressors and push the cylinder block all the way down onto the crankcase.

10. Refer to *Cylinder Head Service — Installation* and continue assembly. Refer to Chapter Two, *Valve Clearance Measurement,* and *Adjusting Valve Clearance* and check the valve adjustment and correct it if necessary. Service and tune the engine as described in Chapter Two.

OIL PUMP

When the engine is warmed up to operating temperature and running at idle, the oil pressure indicator lamp should remain unlit. If it flickers, glows weakly, or lights up completely, the pump discharge pressure may not be sufficient. Have the pressure measured by a dealer. It's a relatively simple check, but it requires an expensive gauge that you may not have occasion to use more than once.

If the discharge pressure is low, remove the pump, inspect, and service it as described below.

Removal/Installation

1. Refer to *Engine Removal/Installation* and carry out Steps 30 through 35.

2. Remove the circlip from the oil pump drive shaft and remove the drive gear (**Figure 88**).

3. Loosen the 3 oil pump retaining screws with an impact driver, unscrew them, and remove the oil pump (**Figure 89**).

4. Install the pump by reversing the above steps. Apply liquid locking compound such as Loctite Lock-N-Seal to the screw threads before tightening them.

Inspection

1. Drive out the pins that hold the oil pump halves together and separate them (**Figure 90**).

2. Measure the clearance between the inner and outer rotors (**Figure 91**). It should be 0.2mm (0.008 in.).

3. Measure the clearance between the outer rotor and the body (**Figure 92**). It should be 0.25mm (0.0098 in.).

4. With a straightedge, measure the rotor side clearance (**Figure 93**). It should be 0.15mm (0.0059 in.).

If any of the above clearances are greater than specified, replace the oil pump as an assembly.

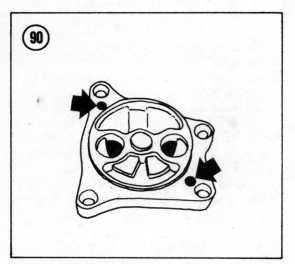

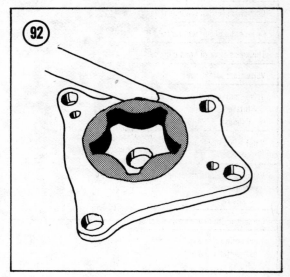

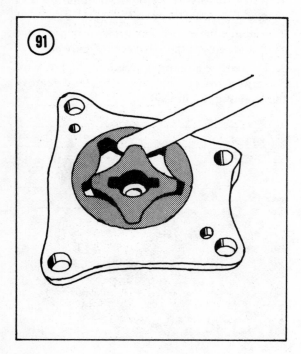

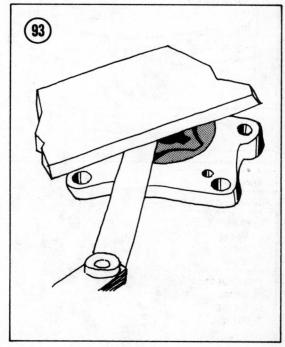

Table 1 SPECIFICATIONS/SERVICE LIMITS

Item	Standard	Service Limit
Cam Height (Base circle + lift) 　　Intake 　　Exhaust	 36.265-36.295mm (1.4278-1.4289 in.) 35.735-35.765mm (1.4069-1.4081 in.)	 36.150mm (1.4232 in.) 35.600mm (1.4016 in.)
Camshaft/journal clearance	0.020-0.054mm (0.0008-0.0021 in.)	0.150mm (0.0059 in.)
Camshaft journal holder inside diameter	21.959-21.980mm (0.8645-0.8654 in.)	_____
Camshaft deflection	0.03mm (0.0012 in.)	0.1mm (0.04 in.)
Cam chain tensioner guide roller wear	_____	2.5mm :0.098 in.)
Cylinder head surface warpage	0.03mm (0.0012 in.)	0.25mm (0.0098 in.)
Thickness of valve head periphery	0.8-1.2mm (0.031-0.047 in.)	0.5mm (0.020 in.)
Valve stem axis runout	_____	0.05mm (0.0020 in.)
Valve stem diameter 　　Intake 　　Exhaust	 6.965-6.980mm (0.2742-0.2748 in.) 6.955-6.970mm (0.2738-0.2744 in.)	 6.90mm (0.2717 in.) 6.805mm (0.2679 in.)
Valve guide inside diameter	7.000-7.015mm (0.2756-0.2762 in.)	Intake: 7.09mm (0.2891 in.) Exhaust: 7.10mm (0.2795 in.)
Valve/valve guide clearance 　　Intake 　　Exhaust	 0.02-0.05mm (0.0008-0.0020 in.) 0.03-0.06mm (0.0012-0.0024 in.)	 0.09mm (0.0035 in.) 0.10mm (0.0039 in.)
Contact width of valve and valve seat	1.0-1.2mm (0.039-0.047 in.)	1.5mm (0.059 in.)
Valve spring free length 　Mihon Hatsujo make 　　Inner 　　Outer 　Chuoh Hatsujo make 　　Inner 　　Outer	 37.00mm (1.457 in.) 43.25mm (1.703 in.) 35.30mm (1.390 in.) 43.00mm (1.693 in.)	 33.8mm (1.331 in.) 41.5mm (1.634 in.) 33.8mm (1.331 in.) 41.5mm (1.634 in.)
Valve spring tension 　Outer 　Inner	 50.4-58.3 kg (111-129 lbs.) for fitting 　length of 27mm (1.06 in.) 29.3-34.0 kg (65-75 lbs.) for fitting 　length of 23mm (0.91 in.)	 _____ _____
Compression pressure	9-12 kg/sq. cm^2 (128-171 psi)	7 kg/sq. cm^2 (100 psi)
Oil pump discharge pressure	Over 0.1 kg/cm^2 (1.42 psi) at 3,000 rpm	_____
Cylinder bore	65.000-65.015mm (2.5591-2.5596 in.)	65.100mm (2.5630 in.)
Piston diameter	64.945-64.960mm (2.5569-2.5575 in.)	64.800mm (2.5512 in.)
Cylinder/piston clearance	0.050-0.060mm (0.0020-0.0024 in.)	_____
Piston ring thickness 　Top ring 　2nd ring 　Oil ring	 1.175-1.190mm (0.0463-0.0469 in.) 1.170-1.190mm (0.0461-0.0469 in.) 2.50mm (0.098 in.)	 1.100mm (0.0433 in.) 1.100mm (0.0433 in.) _____
Piston ring groove width 　Top ring 　2nd ring 　Oil ring	 1.21-1.23mm (0.0476-0.0484 in.) 1.21-1.23mm (0.0476-0.0484 in.) 2.51-2.53mm (0.0988-0.0996 in.)	 1.30mm (0.0512 in.) 1.30mm (0.0512 in.) 2.60mm (0.1024 in.)

(continued)

4

Table 1   SPECIFICATIONS/SERVICE LIMITS (continued)

Item	Standard	Service Limit
Piston ring/ring groove clearance		
Top ring	0.020-0.055mm (0.0008-0.0022 in.)	0.18mm (0.0071 in.)
2nd ring	0.020-0.060mm (0.0008-0.0024 in.)	0.18mm (0.0071 in.)
Oil ring	———	0.15mm (0.0059 in.)
Piston ring end gap		
Top ring	0.1-0.3mm (0.004-0.012 in.)	0.6mm (0.024 in.)
2nd ring	0.1-0.3mm (0.004-0.012 in.)	0.6mm (0.024 in.)
Piston ring free end gap		
Top ring	8mm (0.31 in.)	6mm (0.24 in.)
2nd ring	8mm (0.31 in.)	6mm (0.24 in.)
Piston pin diameter	15.995-16.000mm (0.6297-0.6299 in.)	15.96mm (0.6283 in.)
Piston pin bore	16.008-16.002mm (0.6302-0.6300 in.)	16.08mm (0.6331 in.)
Connecting rod small end bore	16.014-16.006mm (0.6305-0.6302 in.)	16.05mm (0.6319 in.)
Connecting rod deflection	———	3mm (0.12 in.)
Crankshaft bearing diametral clearance	0.015-0.040mm (0.0006-0.0016 in.)	0.08mm (0.0031 in.)
Connecting rod side clearance	0.65-0.10mm (0.026-0.004 in.)	1.0mm (0.04 in.)
Crankshaft runout	Below 0.03mm (0.0012 in.)	0.06mm (0.0024 in.)
Tappet clearance	0.03-0.08mm (0.001-0.003 in.)	———

Table 2   ENGINE TORQUE SPECIFICATIONS

	Bolt Dia. (mm)	Mkg	Ft.-lb.
Clutch sleeve hub nut	24	4.0—6.0	29—43
Drive sprocket nut	20	4.0—6.0	29—43
Starter clutch bolt	8	1.5—2.0	11—14
Contact breaker cam bolt	10	1.8—2.8	13—20
Cam chain tensioner sleeve bolt	24	3.0—3.5	21—25
Cam chain tensioner locknut	6	1.0—1.2	7—8
Camshaft sprocket bolt	6	1.0	7
Cylinder head bolt	6	0.7—1.1	5—8
Cylinder head nut	10	3.5—4.0	25—29
Cylinder head cover bolt	6	0.7—1.1	5—8
Camshaft holder bolt	6	0.8	5.8
Cam chain idler sprocket bolt	6	0.6—1.0	4—7
Oil filter cover nut	6	0.6—0.8	4—5
Oil pan bolt	6	1.0	7
Crankcase bolt	6	1.0	7
Crankcase bolt	8	2.0	14
Engine mounting bolt	10	4.0	29
Engine mounting plate bolt	8	2.0	14
AC generator rotor bolt	12	6.0—7.0	43—50

CHAPTER FIVE

CLUTCH AND TRANSMISSION

CLUTCH

All clutch parts can be removed with the engine in the frame.

Clutch Cable Replacement

1. Remove the clutch adjuster cover (**Figure 1**).

2. Loosen the locknut on the adjuster and run the adjuster in to release tension from the cable (**Figure 2**). Straighten the tab inside the clevis that locks that cable into the clevis and disconnect the cable (**Figure 3**).

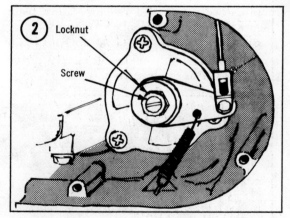

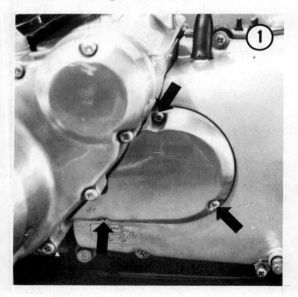

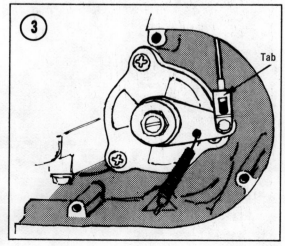

3. Unscrew the adjuster from the case and pull out the cable.

4. Disconnect the cable from the clutch lever (**Figure 4**).

5. Route a new cable alongside the old one, then remove the old cable.

6. Install the cable ends and adjust the clutch as described in Chapter Two, *Clutch Cable*.

Clutch Removal/Installation

1. Completely remove the bolt from the kickstarter lever (**Figure 5**) and pull the lever off the shaft.

2. Loosen the screws in the clutch cover with an impact driver, unscrew them, and remove the cover (**Figure 6**).

3. Shift the transmission into 1st gear. Apply the brake and loosen the clutch bolts in a crisscross pattern (**Figure 7**). Unscrew the bolts, remove the springs and outer pressure plate (**Figure 8**), and the clutch plates (**Figure 9**).

4. Straighten the tab washer on the clutch hub nut and unscrew the nut with an impact driver (**Figure 10**). This can be done without the use of

the special clutch holding tool; wrap the inner hub with a shop rag, have someone hold it, and loosen the nut with the impact driver. Remove the tab washer, the hub, and the thrust washer behind the hub. Notice the grooves in the thrust washer face (**Figure 11**). These must face in when the washer is installed.

5. Install one or two 6mm screws into spacer (**Figure 11**). Pull out on screws and remove spacer, then remove bearing. Shift clutch basket toward rear of engine until primary gear on clutch assembly clears crankcase and remove clutch assembly. Remove oil pump drive gear, bearing, spacer, and washer.

6. Reverse the above to install the clutch. Grease the bearings and races. Torque hub nut to 4.0-6.0 mkg (29-43 ft.-lb.). Make sure dogs oil pump drive gear engage notches in rear of clutch assembly. Grease bearing (**Figure 12**). When installing the plates, begin with a friction plate, then add a metal plate and continue adding plates, alternating friction and metal (**Figures 13 and 14**).

7. Install the throw out bearing hub and inner race (**Figure 15**). Install the needle bearing, lightly oiled (**Figure 16**), and the outer race (**Figure 17**).

8. Install pressure plate and springs (**Figure 18**).

9. Screw in and tighten the bolts in a crisscross pattern (**Figure 19**). Torque to 0.4-0.6 mkg (3-4 ft.-lb.).

10. Adjust the clutch as described in Chapter Two, *Clutch Cable.*

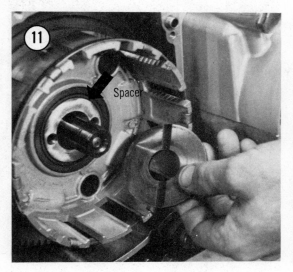

Inspection

1. Measure the free length of the clutch springs **(Figure 20)**. Standard length is 40.4mm (1.59 in.). If they are less than 39mm (1.54 in.), they should be replaced.

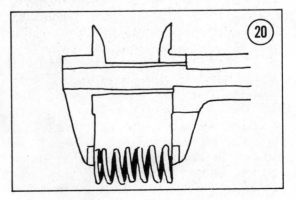

2. Measure the thickness of the friction drive plates (**Figure 21**). Standard is 2.9-3.1mm (0.114-0.122 in.). If they are less than 2.7mm (0.0106 in.), replace them.

3. Measure the distortion of the steel plates (**Figure 22**). If it is greater than 0.3mm (0.012 in.), the plates should be replaced. The plates can be purchased individually, so replace only those that exceed the limit.

TRANSMISSION

The engine must be removed from the motorcycle and the crankcase halves separated to gain access to the transmission. Refer to *Engine Removal/Installation* in Chapter Four and remove the engine using the abbreviated procedure. In addition to the steps listed (1-13, 26-30, and 37-40), it is necessary to perform Steps 31 through 36. Then refer to *Bottom End Disassembly/Assembly* in Chapter Four and separate the crankcase halves.

Before removing the gearsets from the transmission housing, measure the backlash of each of the gears with a dial indicator (**Figure 23**). Standard and service limit specifications are shown in **Table 1**. Record the actual lash to determine which gears should be replaced, if any.

Disassembly

1. Remove the kickstarter drive shaft assembly from the case (**Figure 24**).

2. Remove 2 gearsets — mainshaft assembly and countershaft assembly (**Figure 25**).

3. There is no need to remove the shifting forks unless inspection indicates that they should be replaced. Check them for galling (**Figure 26**). Measure their thickness (**Figure 27**) and replace them if they are less than the service limit of 4.85mm (0.191 in.). Remove them by sliding the fork pivots out the side of the case. Note that the 2 rear forks are identical and differ from the forward fork (**Figure 28**).

4. Inspect the pathways in the shift drum for wear and chips at the corners (**Figure 29**). To remove the drum, first remove the shifter quadrant, then unscrew the Phillips head screws on the retainer plate with an impact

Table 1   GEAR BACKLASH

Gear	Standard	Service Limit
1st, 2nd, 3rd	0-0.04mm (0-0.002 in.)	0.1mm (0.004 in.)
4th, 5th	0.05-0.1mm (0.0019-0.004 in.)	0.15mm (0.006 in.)

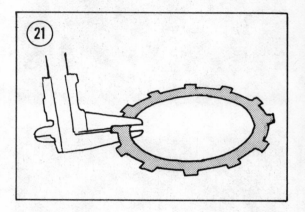

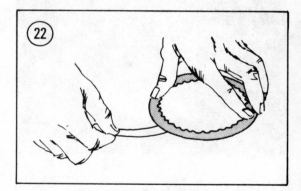

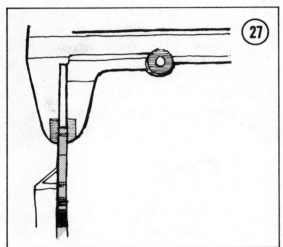

5

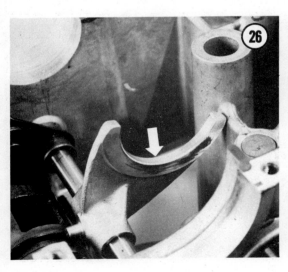

driver and pull the drum out through the right side of the case (**Figure 30**).

5. Check the shift drum detent spring for resiliency (**Figure 31**).

Mainshaft Disassembly/Assembly

Refer to **Figure 32** for this procedure.

1. Press the bearing off the left end of the shaft.

2. Slide off 2nd drive gear, 5th drive gear, and third drive gear.

3. Remove the circlip and washer that retain 4th drive gear, then slide it off the shaft.

4. Reverse the above to assemble the mainshaft gearset.

Countershaft Disassembly/Assembly

Refer to **Figure 33** for this procedure.

1. Remove the seal from the sprocket end of the shaft (**Figure 34**). Press off the bearing (**Figure 35**).

2. Press off the bearing from the opposite end of the shaft. See **Figure 36**.

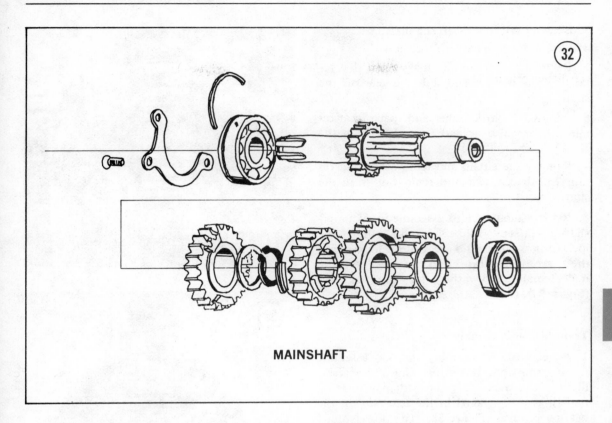

MAINSHAFT

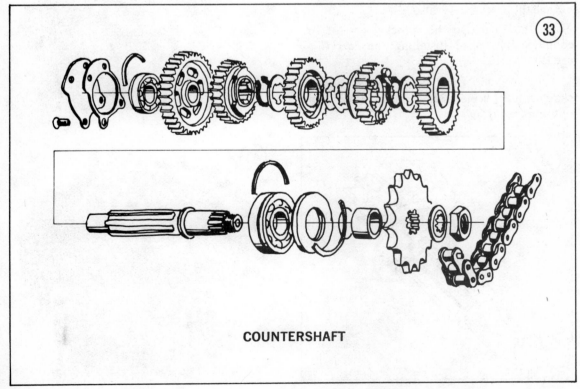

COUNTERSHAFT

3. Slide 1st driven gear off the shaft.

4. Slide 4th driven gear off the shaft.

5. Remove the circlip and lockwasher that retain 3rd driven gear and slide the gear off the shaft.

6. Remove the lockwasher and spacer that retain 5th driven gear and remove it from the shaft.

7. Remove the circlip and lockwasher that retain 2nd driven gear and remove it from the shaft.

8. Reverse the above to assemble the countershaft gearset. Make certain that the lockwashers and circlip are securely locked into their grooves. Also check to see that the male/female lockwasher set are engaged (**Figure 37**).

Transmission Assembly

1. Reverse the disassembly steps to assemble the transmission. When installing the gearsets in the case, make sure the end play locating half-rings are engaged in the case and in the bearing grooves (**Figure 38**). The dowels must engage the case recesses also.

2. Fit the O-ring to the sprocket end of the countershaft before installing the seal (**Figure 39**).

3. Install the left end bearing on the countershaft with the sealed side of the bearing facing out (**Figure 40**).

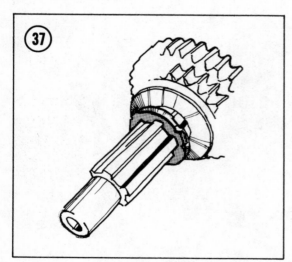

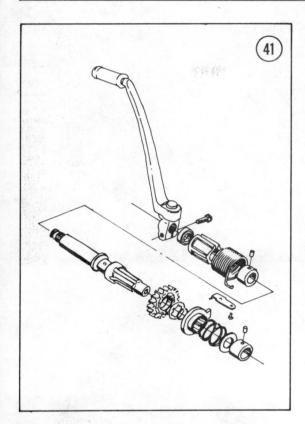

4. Refer to **Figure 41** to assemble the kickstarter assembly. Line up the 2 punch marks when installing the drive arm (**Figure 42**).

5. Install the shift quadrant with the master and slave quadrants centered (**Figure 43**). The spring ends on the master quadrant must straddle the post.

5

CHAPTER SIX

FUEL AND EXHAUST SYSTEMS

The fuel system consists of the fuel tank, control valve and filter, 4 carburetors, and an air cleaner.

The exhaust system consists of 4 head pipes and 2 mufflers.

This chapter includes service procedures for all parts of the fuel and exhaust systems.

AIR CLEANER

The air cleaner element should be cleaned and reoiled every 3,000 miles.

1. Remove the air cleaner cover (**Figure 1**).

2. Remove the screw that holds the air cleaner element in place (**Figure 2**) and pull out the element.

3. Remove the filter from the filter body and wash it in solvent. Squeeze out the solvent by pressing on the filter. *Do not twist it to wring it out.*

4. Soak the filter in engine oil and then press out the excess.

5. Install the filter on the filter body, screw in and tighten the screws, then insert the filter in the air box. Screw in and tighten the retaining screw and install the outer cover.

CARBURETORS

Removal/Installation

1. Raise the seat and unscrew the rear fuel tank mounting bolt (**Figure 3**).

2. Turn the fuel tap to ON or RESERVE and disconnect the fuel line from the carburetor.

3. Slide the tank back and off from the rubber mounts.

4. Unscrew the bolt that attaches the air cleaner box to the frame (**Figure 4**).

5. Loosen the clamping bands between the carburetors and the air cleaner box (**Figure 5**). Disconnect the hoses from the carburetors and remove the air cleaner.

6. Loosen the locknuts on the throttle cable adjusters (**Figure 6**), screw in the adjusters to release tension from the cables, and disconnect the cables from the quadrant.

7. Loosen the clamping bands between the carburetors and the engine (**Figure 7**). Pull rearward to disconnect the carburetors from the engine and remove them from the motorcycle as an assembly. Pull them out carefully so the vent hoses will not be disconnected.

6

8. Installation is the reverse of the procedures above. Route the vent hoses down between the rear of the engine and the swinging arm pivot. When the installation is complete, refer to Chapter Two, *Engine Tune-Up*, and adjust the cables and carburetors and synchronize them.

Disassembly

1. Remove the caps from the carburetors (**Figure 8**).

2. Unscrew the lifter lockbolt from each carburetor (**Figure 9**). Unscrew the lifter quadrant bolt.

3. Remove the rubber plugs from the outer carburetors (**Figure 10**).

4. Unscrew the Allen screw from the throttle rod lock (**Figure 11**). This lock prevents the rod from moving from side to side. Remove the throttle shaft.

5. Unscrew the flush screws that attach the carburetors to the manifold plate (**Figure 12**). Remove the carburetors from the plate. The throttle quadrant and choke lifter mechanism can be left in place on the plate.

6

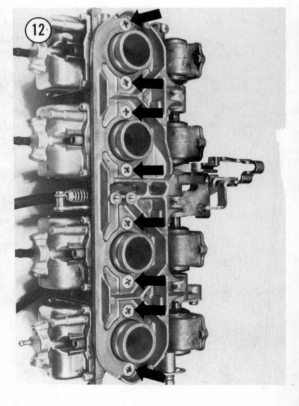

6. Unscrew the screws from the float chamber and remove it (**Figure 13**). Note the sediment trap in the bottom of the float chamber (**Figure 14**). These traps can be cleaned with the carburetors installed on the engine. See Chapter Two.

7. Remove the throttle shaft bushings from the carburetors (**Figure 15**).

8. Remove the float pin and float (**Figure 16**).

9. Unscrew the float needle valve (**Figure 17**) and remove the needle valve.

10. Unscrew the mainjet and the needle valve (**Figure 18**).

6

11. Unscrew the pilot jet **(Figure 19)**.

> CAUTION
> *Do not unscrew or even turn the small jet that is marked with a colored paint seal. This jet is preset at the factory. The position of this jet is calibrated for each individual carburetor and if disturbed, carburetor adjustment can be severely affected. (See Figure 20).*

12. Remove the slide and slide lifter from the carburetor **(Figure 21)** and unscrew the 2 screws that attach the lifter to the slide.

13. Remove the needle from the slide and note the position of the E-clip on the needle **(Figure 22)**. Most likely, the E-clip will be in the center groove, but no matter which position it is in, it should be located in the same position from which it was removed if the carburetor adjustment is correct at the time they are disassembled.

14. Unscrew the idle air screw **(Figure 23)**.

15. Unscrew the choke mechanism **(Figure 24)**.

16. Remove the fuel manifold pipe that connects the carburetor float chamber to the chamber of the adjacent carburetor. Carefully remove the O-rings **(Figure 25)**.

Inspection

1. Soak all of the metal components in carburetor cleaning solution. This solution is available through automotive parts and supply stores, in a small resealable tank with a dip basket for just a few dollars **(Figure 26)**. If it is tightly sealed when not in use it will last for several carburetor rebuilds.

> CAUTION
> *Do not put non-metallic parts such as floats, gaskets, and O-rings in the solution. It may attack them and render them useless.*

2. Check the slides and slide bores for wear. Generally, many thousands of miles of use are necessary before this sort of wear is apparent.

3. Blow out the jets with compressed air. *Do not use wire or sharp instruments to clean them.* They can be easily burred and very likely their sizes will be altered.

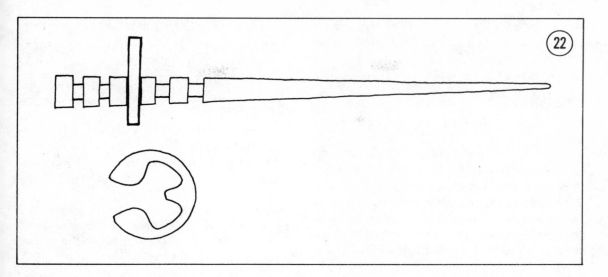

6

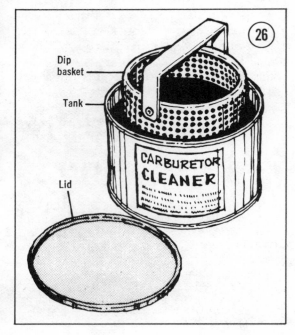

Dip basket

Tank

Lid

CARBURETOR CLEANER

4. Inspect all of the O-rings for damage or deterioration and replace any that are less than perfect.

Assembly

1. Assembly is the reverse of the disassembly procedure. After installing the needle in the slide, position the slide lifter so that the third hole in the slide lifter lines up with the third hole in the slide (**Figure 27**).

2. When installing the slide and lifter assembly in the carburetor, make certain the needle fits in the needle jet and the lug in the body lines up with the groove in the slide (**Figure 28**).

FUEL PETCOCK

Replacement

1. Drain the fuel tank into a safe, sealable container.

2. Disconnect the lines from the petcock (**Figure 29**). Remove the petcock from the tank.

3. Before installing the petcock, clean the screen thoroughly.

EXHAUST SYSTEM

The exhaust system consists of four head pipes and two 2-into-1 mufflers.

Head Pipe
Removal/Installation

1. Loosen the clamp that holds the head pipe in the muffler (**Figure 30**).

2. Unscrew the nuts from the head pipe collar (**Figure 31**) and pull the head pipe out of the muffler.

3. Installation is the reverse of the above. If 2 or more pipes are removed at the same time, identify them for location with the letters stamped on them (**Figure 32**).

Muffler
Removal/Installation

1. Loosen the clamps that hold the head pipes in the muffler (**Figure 33**).

2. Unscrew the bolts that mount the muffler to the frame (**Figure 34**) and pull back on the muffler to release it from the head pipes.

3. Installation is the reverse of the procedures above.

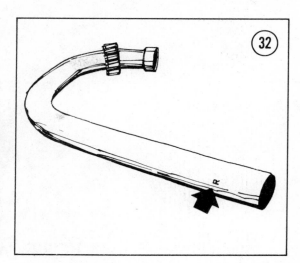

6

CHAPTER SEVEN

ELECTRICAL SYSTEM

The electrical system includes the following subsystems:

a. Charging system
b. Starting system
c. Ignition system
d. Switches and lamps

CHARGING SYSTEM

The charging system consists of the battery, alternator, rectifier, and regulator (**Figure 1**).

The alternator generates an alternating current (AC) which the the rectifier converts to direct current (DC). The regulator maintains the voltage going to the battery and the load (lights, ignition, etc.) at a constant voltage regardless of variations in engine speed and load.

Testing

Whenever a charging system trouble is suspected, make sure the battery is fully charged and in good condition before beginning (see *Battery*). Also make certain all connections are clean and tight.

1. Raise the seat. Refer to **Figure 2** and disconnect the *yellow* wire from the regulator to isolate it from the circuit.

2. Connect the *white/green* wire from the alternator to the *white/red* wire from the rectifier.

3. Make sure all lights are switched off (this is a no-load test). Start the engine, allow it to warm up, and then bring its speed up to 5,000 rpm and hold it at that point. With a voltmeter, check the output of the *red* wire from the rectifier. If the line voltage is 17 volts or higher the alternator and rectifier are all right. If the voltage is less than 17 volts, either the alternator or rectifier or both are unsatisfactory. If the voltage is satisfactory, check the regulator for performance as described in the next step. If it is not satisfactory, test the alternator and rectifier as described below.

4. Shut off the engine and reconnect the wiring in the normal manner. Make sure that the light switch is turned off. Start the engine, bring its speed up to 5,000 rpm and hold it at that point. With a voltmeter, check the line voltage from the regulator. If the voltage is 14-15.5 volts, the voltage regulator is all right. If the voltage is less than 14 volts or more than 15.5 volts, the regulator is unsatisfactory and should be replaced.

> NOTE: *For U.S. and Canadian models, remove the headlamp switch lock cap and turn off the headlamp (Figure 3) for this test.*

Alternator Test

1. Disconnect the alternator leads (**Figure 4**)

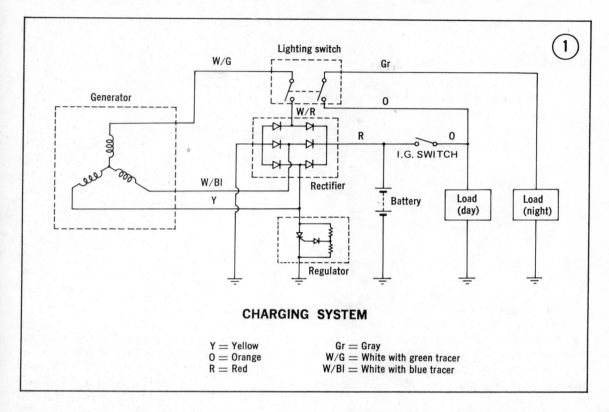

CHARGING SYSTEM

Y = Yellow   Gr = Gray
O = Orange   W/G = White with green tracer
R = Red   W/Bl = White with blue tracer

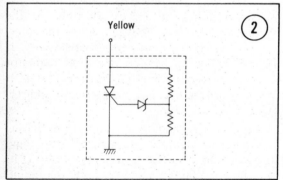

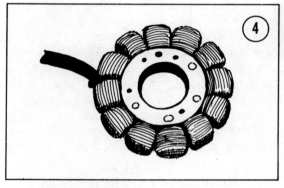

and check the continuity between each pair of wires (*white/green* and *white/black; white/green* and *yellow;* and *white/black* and *yellow).*

2. In each case the resistance should be 60-70 ohms. If it is less than 60 ohms in any hookup (open stator winding) or greater than 70 ohms in any hookup, (shorted stator winding), replace the stator.

CAUTION
Both Denso and Kokusan alternators are used on the GS750; the components are not interchangeable. Make certain

the new stator is the same make as the rotor.

Rectifier Test

The 6 diodes in the rectifier are the electrical equivalent of one-way valves; they permit current to flow in a forward direction and prevent it from flowing in the reverse direction — if they are functioning correctly.

> CAUTION
> *A circuit tester must be used for this test; do not use a megger instrument. Its internal power supply can and most likely will destroy otherwise good diodes.*

1. Disconnect all of the leads to the rectifier (**Figure 5**).
2. Touch the tester's negative probe to the ground terminal (*black/white*). Touch the positive probe first to the *yellow* wire, then the *white/red* wire, then the *white/blue*. In each case continuity should be indicated. If not, the rectifier is faulty and must be replaced. If continuity is present in each case, proceed with the next step.
3. Switch the probes — positive probe to the *black/white* wire and negative probe to the *yellow, white/red,* and *white/blue* wires in turn. With this hookup, there should be no continuity. If continuity is indicated, the rectifier is faulty and should be replaced. If there is no continuity, check the other 3 diodes, using the *red* wire as the ground, first with the negative probe on the *red* and then the positive. If any of the diodes is faulty, the rectifier must be replaced.

> CAUTION
> *Do not run the engine with the rectifier leads disconnected; the alternator is certain to be damaged.*

STARTING SYSTEM

The starting system consists of the components shown in **Figure 6**. Before checking for suspected trouble in the starting system, make certain all connections are clean and tight. Make certain also that the battery is in good condition, with correct electrolyte level, and fully charged.

If the system is functioning correctly, the relay (**Figure 7**) will make a single audible "clack" when the starter button is pressed and the motor will begin to turn at once.

If the relay makes no sound, and the motor does not turn, and if the battery is fully charged, an open circuit in the relay coil is likely. It must be replaced.

If the relay chatters when the button is pressed, and the motor does not turn, there may be a bad ground connection, the relay contacts may be faulty, or the motor may have an internal open circuit. In such a case, the problem should be referred to a dealer for thorough testing.

BATTERY

Care and Inspection

1. Raise the seat and disconnect the battery hold-down strap (**Figure 8**).
2. Disconnect the battery terminals — ground first then the positive (**Figure 9**). Remove the battery from the box.
3. Clean the top of the battery with a solution of baking soda and water. Scrub off any stubborn deposits with a wire brush and rinse the battery with clear water. Dry it thoroughly.

> CAUTION
> *Keep cleaning solution out of the battery cells or the electrolyte will be severely weakened.*

4. Clean the battery leads with a stiff wire brush.
5. Inspect the battery case for cracks. If any are found, the battery should be replaced. Its condition will deteriorate rapidly and leaking electrolyte could damage painted, plated, and polished surfaces as well as electrical insulation.
6. If the battery is in good condition, install it and connect the leads, positive first then ground.
7. Coat the terminals with petroleum jelly, such as Vaseline.
8. Check the electrolyte level and correct it if necessary. Add only distilled water, never electrolyte.

Testing

Hydrometer testing is the best way to check

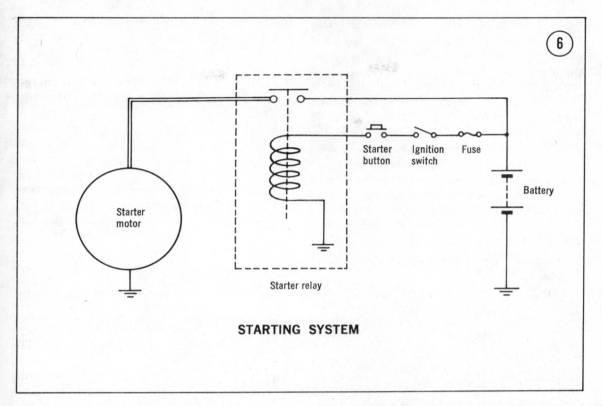

STARTING SYSTEM

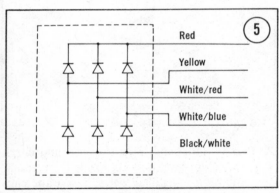

battery condition. Use a hydrometer with numbered graduations from 1.100 to 1.300 rather than one with color-coded bands. To use the hydrometer, squeeze the rubber ball, insert the tip in the cell and release the ball. Draw enough electrolyte to float the weighted float inside the hydrometer. Note the number in line with surface of the electrolyte; this is the specific gravity for this cell. Return the electrolyte to the cell from which it came.

The specific gravity of the electrolyte in each battery cell is an excellent indication of that cell's condition. A fully charged cell will read 1.275-1.380, while a cell in good condition may read from 1.250-1.280. A cell in fair condition reads from 1.225-1.250 and anything below 1.225 is practically dead.

Specific gravity varies with temperature. For each 10° that electrolyte temperature exceeds 80°F, add 0.004 to reading indicated on hydrometer. Subtract 0.004 for each 10° below 80°F.

If the cells test in the poor range, the battery requires recharging. The hydrometer is useful for checking the progress of the charging operation. **Table 1** shows approximate state of charge.

Table 1   STATE OF CHARGE

Specific Gravity	State of Charge
1.110-1.130	Discharged
1.140-1.160	Almost discharged
1.170-1.190	One-quarter charged
1.200-1.220	One-half charged
1.230-1.250	Three-quarters charged
1.260-1.280	Fully charged

CAUTION
Always disconnect both battery connections before connecting charging equipment.

Charging

The battery can be charged while installed in the motorcycle; however, it is so easily removed after the leads have been disconnected it is not worth the risk of damaging the motorcycle

finish with electrolyte during charging.

Charge it only in a well-ventilated area.

WARNING
Make certain open flame and cigarettes, etc., are kept away from the battery during charging. Highly explosive hydrogen gas is formed during charging. And never arc the terminals to check the condition of charge; the resulting spark could ignite the gas.

1. Connect the charger — positive-to-positive and negative-to-negative. See **Figure 10**.

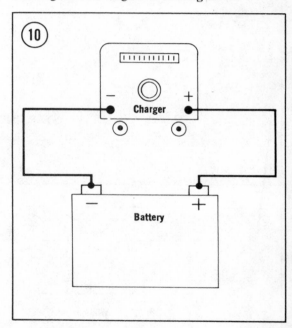

2. Remove the caps from the cells and check the electrolyte level and correct it if necessary by adding only distilled water. Leave the caps off during charging.

3. If the charger output is variable, select a low rate (1.5-3 amps), turn on the charger and allow the battery to charge as long as possible. If it is severely discharged, as long as 8 hours may be required to charge it completely.

4. When charging is complete, test it with a hydrometer as described above. If the specific gravity level is satisfactory, wait an hour and test it again. If the level is still correct, the battery is fully charged and in good condition. If the specific gravity level drops between tests, it is likely that one or more cells are sulfated. In

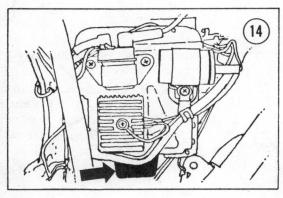

such a case, the battery should be replaced as soon as possible.

COMPONENT REPLACEMENT

CAUTION
Before removing any of the components described below, disconnect the battery leads.

Stator Removal/Installation

1. Remove the left side engine cover **(Figure 11)**. Disconnect the stator leads **(Figure 12)** and loosen the clamps that retain the harness.

2. Unscrew the screws that attach the stator to the case and remove it.

3. Installation is the reverse. Make certain the harness is correctly routed and the clips are secure.

Rotor Removal/Installation

A special puller is required to remove the rotor; however, the likelihood of a malfunction in the rotor is very remote. Should its removal be required, it is recommended that the job be entrusted to a dealer. The cost will doubtless be less than the cost of the special puller.

Rectifier Removal/Installation

1. Remove the left side cover.

2. Disconnect the rectifier leads. Unscrew the rectifier attaching screw and remove the unit.

3. Installation is the reverse. Make certain the leads are connected as shown in **Figure 13**.

Regulator Removal/Installation

1. Remove the left side cover.

2. Disconnect the regulator lead and unscrew the attaching screws **(Figure 14)**. Remove the regulator.

3. Installation is the reverse. Make sure the screws are tight and the lead connection is clean and tight.

Starter Relay
Removal/Installation

1. Remove the left side cover.

2. Disconnect the lead from the relay. Unscrew

the 2 attaching screws (**Figure 15**) and remove the relay.

3. Installation is the reverse. Make sure the screws are tight to ensure a good ground. Make sure the electrical connection is clean and tight.

Starter Removal/Installation

1. Remove the left engine cover.

2. Remove the starter cover (**Figure 16**) and disconnect the starter lead.

3. Unscrew the bolts that attach the starter to the engine (**Figure 17**).

4. Pull the starter out of the case and collect the drive gear and spacers.

5. Installation is the reverse. Make certain that there is a spacer behind and in front of the starter gear. Make sure the starter lead connection is clean and tight, as well as the mounting bolts to ensure a good ground.

IGNITION SYSTEM

The ignition system consists of 2 coils, 2 contact breaker sets and condensers on a single plate, and 4 spark plugs (**Figure 18**).

Basic ignition work, such as that performed during a tune-up, is presented in this Chapter Two. The procedures presented in this chapter cover removal/installation of the ignition coils and testing of the coils and condensers.

IGNITION COILS

Removal/Installation

The coils are located beneath the fuel tank.

1. Raise the seat and unscrew the rear tank mounting bolt (**Figure 19**).

2. Turn the fuel tap to ON or RES. Disconnect the fuel line at the carburetor and pull the tank back to disconnect it from the rubber front mounts.

> NOTE: *Before installing the fuel tank, lubricate the rubber front mounts with rubber lube or WD-40 to aid installation and removal later on.*

3. Disconnect the primary leads from the coils. Note that the double *orange/white* lead from each coil is the primary side and is connected to

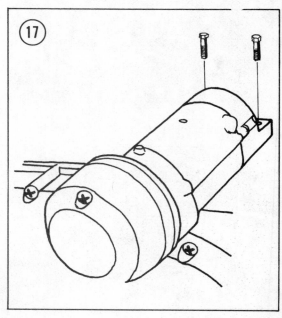

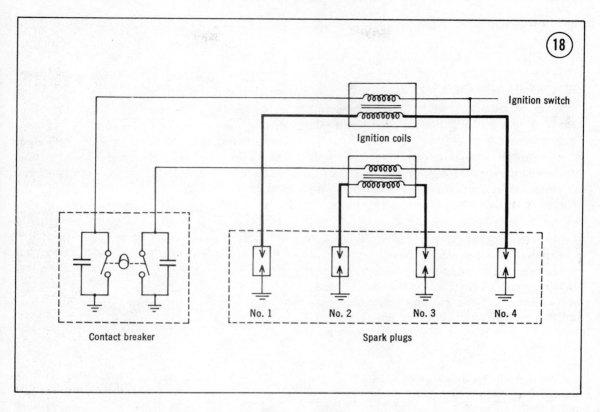

Ignition switch

Ignition coils

Contact breaker

Spark plugs

No. 1   No. 2   No. 3   No. 4

7

the ignition switch. See wiring diagram at the end of this chapter.

4. Disconnect the high-tension leads from the spark plug — grasp the spark plug caps, not the wires, to pull them off.

5. Unscrew the nuts from the coil mounts and remove them along with high-tension leads **(Figure 20)**.

6. Installation is the reverse of these steps. Make sure the the high-tension leads are routed to their respective cylinders. The wires are marked with the appropriate cylinder number. number.

Testing

The only certain test for a suspected coil is to replace it with a coil that is known to be good. For instance, if 2 of the cylinders are operating satisfactorily (either 1 and 4 or 2 and 3) interchange the coils and see if the symptoms move to the opposite pair of cylinders.

CONDENSERS

The condensers can be tested with an ohmmeter equipped with a battery of 12 volts or less. An ohmmeter equipped with a battery of higher output will destroy a good condenser as soon as it is connected.

1. Connect one lead of the ohmmeter to the metal case of the condenser.

2. Touch the other ohmmeter lead to the condenser lead. If the condenser is good, the ohmmeter will at first indicate a very low resistance, then start climbing higher and higher. It may reach infinity. Touch the condenser lead to the case to discharge it.

3. If the meter drops to a low value and stays there, or climbs only slightly, the condenser is shorted. If the needle never drops to a low value, but remains high, the condenser is open. In either case, replace the condenser.

BREAKER POINTS

Breaker point maintenance is fully described in Chapter Two.

SPARK PLUGS

Spark plug maintenance is fully described in Chapter Two.

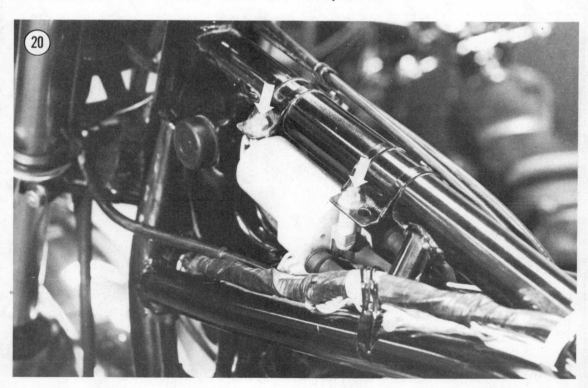

LIGHTING SYSTEM

The lighting system consists of the headlamp (with 2 filaments for high-beam and low-beam operation), the taillamp, stoplamp, directional signals, and warning and indicator lamps. **Table 2** lists replacement bulbs for these components.

Headlamp Replacement

1. Loosen the lockscrew at the top of the headlamp rim (**Figure 21**) and pull the rim out from the top.

2. Unplug the connector from the rear of the headlamp.

3. Remove the clips that lock the lamp into the rim (**Figure 22**) and remove the lamp.

4. Installation is the reverse of the above. Adjust the headlamp beam as described below.

Headlamp Adjustment

Adjust the headlamp beam horizontally and vertically according to the motor vehicle regulations in your area.

To adjust it horizontally, turn the screw (**Figure 23**). To adjust it vertically, loosen the

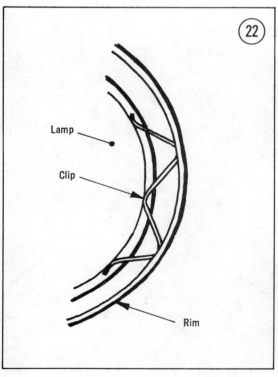

Lamp

Clip

Rim

7

Table 2   LAMP RATINGS

	Watts
Headlamp*	
High beam	50
Low beam	40
Meter lamp	3.4
Turn signal indicator lamp	3.4
High beam indicator lamp	3.4
Oil pressure indicator lamp	3.4
Neutral indicator lamp	3.4
Turn signal lamp	23
Rear combination lamps	
Tail and parking	8 (3 cp)
Stop	23 (32 cp)

*U.S. and Canadian models use a 50/35 watt
sealed beam unit.

mounting bolts on either side (**Figure 24**), move the headlight body as required, and tighten the bolts without further moving the headlight body.

Taillamp Replacement

A single bulb functions as a taillamp, stoplamp, and license plate illumination lamp.

If only one of the 2 filaments fail, the bulb must be replaced. To replace it, remove the lens and turn the bulb counterclockwise to unlock it, clockwise to lock the new bulb into the socket.

Direetional Signal
Lamp Replacement

To replace any of the 4 directional signal lamps, remove the lens, turn the bulb counterclockwise to unlock it, and turn the new bulb clockwise to lock it into the socket. When installing the lens, do not tighten the screws so tightly that the lens cracks.

Front Stoplamp
Switch Replacement

The front stoplamp switch is operated by the brake lever when the brake is applied. Refer to **Figure 25** for this procedure.

1. Remove 2 screws securing switch cover to brake lever assembly.

2. Carefully lift off switch housing. Do not lose the spring-loaded switch contact in the switch body. Replace brass switch contact if worn.

24

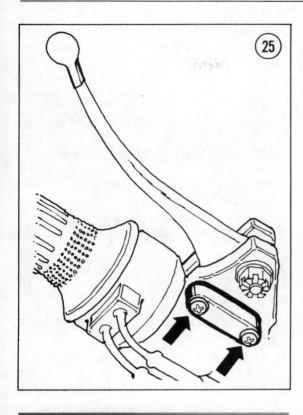

3. Installation is the reverse of these steps. Make sure small spring is installed beneath brass contact.

Rear Stoplamp Switch Replacment

1. Disconnect the wires from the switch (**Figure 26**).

2. Unscrew the locknut from the switch barrel and remove the switch from the bracket. Disconnect it from the pull spring.

3. Installation is the reverse of these steps. Adjust it by raising the switch body in the bracket to make it turn on earlier or lowering the switch body to make it turn on later.

Directional Lamp Relay Replacement

1. Remove the left side cover.

2. Unscrew the mounting screw (**Figure 27**), pull the relay out and disconnect the wires.

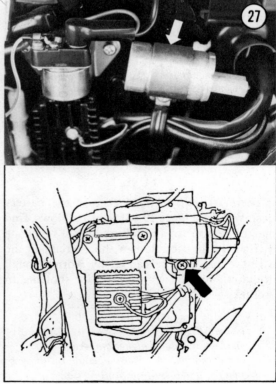

7

3. Connect the wires to a new relay. Disconnect one wire from the old relay and connect it to the new relay before connecting the next wire to ensure that they are not inadvertently switched.

Horn Removal/Installation

1. Disconnect the wires from the horn.
2. Remove the bolts that attach the horn to the frame.
3. Installation is the reverse of these steps.

Horn Testing

1. Disconnect the wires from the horn.
2. Connect jumper wires between a 12-volt battery and the horn terminals. If the horn sounds, it is all right. Check the continuity of the switch.

Horn Switch
Removal/Installation

The horn switch is part of the directional signal control switch assembly. If it is faulty, the entire unit must be replaced.

Direction Switch
Removal/Installation

1. Disconnect the directional signals and horn wires.
2. Remove the mirror from the switch housing.
3. Remove the screws from the switch body (**Figure 28**), separate the halves of the switch.
4. Installation is the reverse of these steps.

FUSE

There is a single main fuse in the battery positive lead (**Figure 29**). If the fuse blows, find out the reason for the failure before replacing it. Usually the trouble is a short-circuit in the wiring. This may be caused by worn-through insulation or a disconnected wire shorting to ground.

> CAUTION
> *Never substitute tinfoil or wire for a fuse. Never user a higher amperage fuse than specified. An overload could result in a fire and loss of the motorcycle.*

WIRING DIAGRAM

A wiring diagram for the GS750 is included at the end of this chapter.

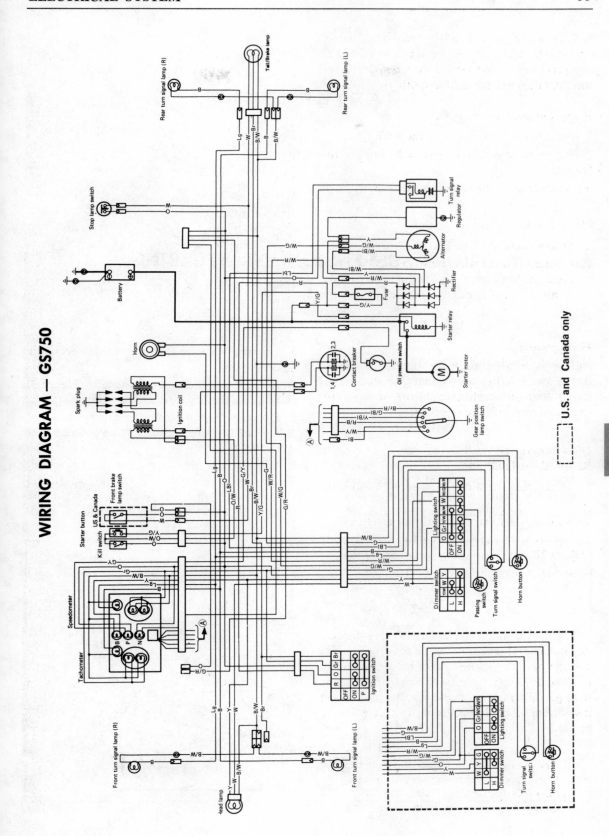

WIRING DIAGRAM — GS750

U.S. and Canada only

CHAPTER EIGHT

FRONT SUSPENSION AND STEERING

This chapter includes repair, replacement, and service procedures for the front wheel, forks, and steering components. Work involving the front brake is presented in Chapter Ten.

FRONT WHEEL

Removal/Installation

1. Place the motorcycle on the centerstand and support the engine with a block (**Figure 1**) so the front wheel is clear of the ground.

2. Unscrew the speedometer cable from the wheel (**Figure 2**).

3. Remove cotter key from the axle (**Figure 3**) and discard the key. Loosen the axle nut.

4. Unscrew the nuts from the axle holders and pull them off their studs. Remove the wheel from the forks.

5. Reverse the above to install the wheel. Tighten the axle holder nuts evenly to 1.5-2.5 mkg (11-18 ft.-lb.). The gaps between the end of the forks and the holders should be equal

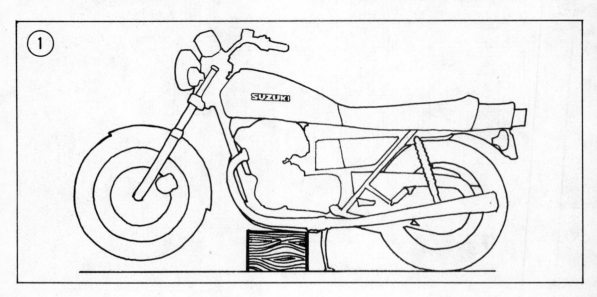

(Figure 4). Tighten the axle nut to 3.6-5.2 mkg (26-38 ft.-lb.).

6. Turn the wheel by hand and make sure that it turns smoothly. Apply the brake several times and check again for smooth rotation and clearance between the disc and pads. If the outer pad drags on the disc, loosen the axle holder nuts on the left fork and pull the fork leg away from the disc a slight amount. Then retighten the nuts. If the inner pad drags on the disc, push inward slightly on the fork leg and tighten the holder nuts.

Disassembly

1. Refer to **Figure 5** for this procedure. Unscrew the axle nut and remove the axle and the speedometer drive.

2. Straighten the lock tabs on the disc bolts. Unscrew the bolts and remove the disc. Remove the right bearing cover.

3. Tap the bearings out of the hub with a long, soft drift. Collect the spacers.

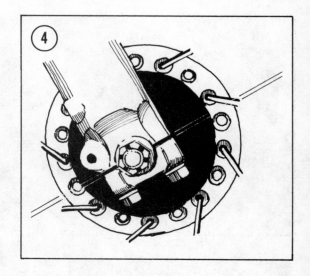

Inspection

1. Inspect the brake components as described in Chapter Ten.

2. Clean the hub inside and out with solvent. Clean the bearing covers, the axle, and the

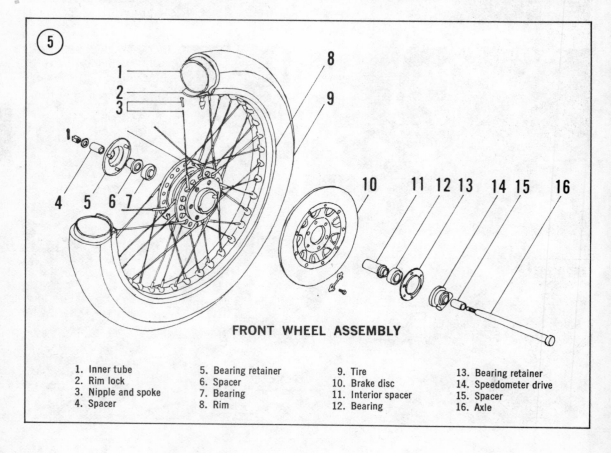

FRONT WHEEL ASSEMBLY

1. Inner tube	5. Bearing retainer	9. Tire	13. Bearing retainer
2. Rim lock	6. Spacer	10. Brake disc	14. Speedometer drive
3. Nipple and spoke	7. Bearing	11. Interior spacer	15. Spacer
4. Spacer	8. Rim	12. Bearing	16. Axle

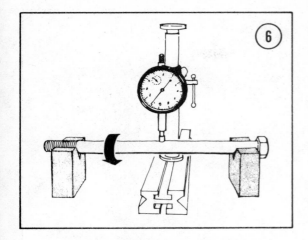

speedometer drive. Clean the spacers inside and out.

CAUTION
Do not clean the bearings in solvent. They are sealed and permanently lubricated.

3. Turn each bearing by hand and check it for smoothness and play. It should turn smoothly and quietly. Replace the bearings if they are questionable.

4. Inspect the axle for runout (**Figure 6**). If it exceeds 0.25 mm (0.010 in.), replace the axle. *Do not attempt to straighten it.*

Assembly

1. Refer to **Figure 5**. Pack the inside of the hub with grease. Grease the spacers inside and out.

2. Install the left bearing in the hub using a driver or socket that is only fractionally smaller in diameter than the outer bearing race. This is essential so that the force required to drive the bearing into the hub is applied only to the outer race.

3. Install the interior spacer through the inside of the hub. The shoulder on the spacer rests against the left bearing inner race.

4. Install the right bearing, spacer, and bearing retainer.

5. Install the disc. Tighten the bolts to 1.5-2.5 mkg (11-18 ft.-lb.) and bend the lock tabs over against the flats on the bolt heads.

6. Install the speedometer drive so that the tangs on the drive unit line up with the slots in the hub (**Figure 7**). Refer to *Removal/Installation* and install the wheel.

Wheel Balancing

An unbalanced wheel can be dangerous. Depending on the degree of unbalance and speed, the rider may experience anything from mild vibration to violent shimmy. In severe cases, the rider can lose control.

Wheels are relatively easy to balance without special equipment. Your dealer has an assortment of balance weights which attach to the spokes. They are crimped onto the light side of the wheel with ordinary gas pliers (**Figure 8**).

8

Buy a couple of each weight available (**Figure 9**). If they are undamaged, you can return the unused weights.

> NOTE: *The "adhesive type" balance weights for alloy wheels are available from most auto tire dealers.*

Before balancing the wheel make sure the bearings are in good condition and properly lubricated.

1. Support the ends of the axle so the wheel can turn freely (**Figure 10**).

2. Rotate the wheel slowly and allow it to come to rest by itself. Make a chalk mark on the tire

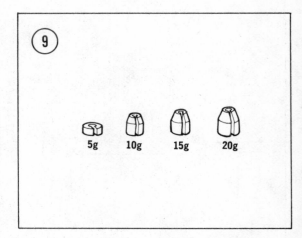

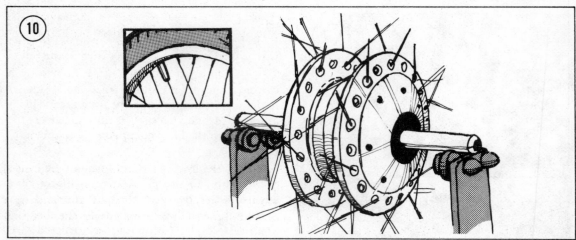

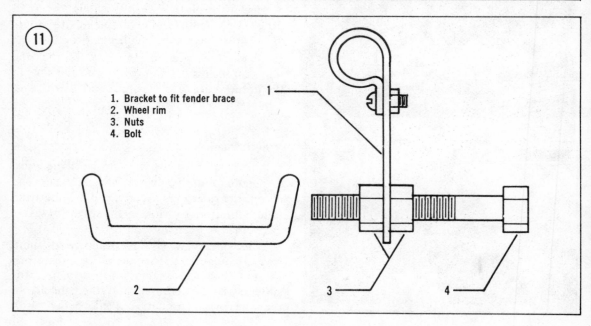

1. Bracket to fit fender brace
2. Wheel rim
3. Nuts
4. Bolt

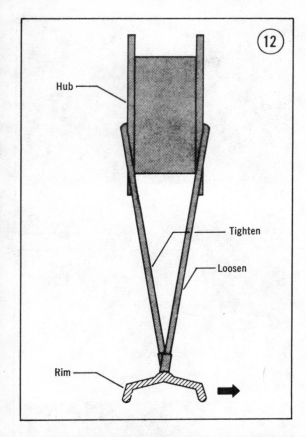

at the 6 o'clock position and rotate the wheel as before, several times, noting the position of the chalk mark each time the wheel comes to rest. If it stops at different positions each time, the wheel is balanced.

3. If the chalk mark stops at the same position — 6 o'clock — each time, add weight to the 12 o'clock position until the chalk mark stops at a different position each time.

4. Install the wheel and road test the motorcycle on a smooth, straight road.

Spoke Adjustment

Spokes loosen with use and should be checked periodically. If all appear loose, tighten all spokes on one side of the hub, then tighten all the spokes on the other side. One-half to one turn should be sufficient; don't overtighten. If you have a torque spoke wrench, tighten spokes to 17-38 in.-lb. (0.2-0.45 mkg).

After tightening spokes, check rim runout to be sure you haven't pulled the rim out of shape.

One way to check rim runout is to mount a dial indicator on the front fork so that it bears on the rim.

If you don't have a dial indicator, improvise as shown in **Figure 11**. Adjust position of bolt until it just clears rim. Rotate rim and note whether clearance increases or decreases. Mark the tire with chalk or crayon at areas that produce significantly large or small clearance. Clearance must not change by more than 0.08 in. (2mm).

To pull rim out, tighten spokes which terminate on the same side of hub and loosen spokes which terminate on opposite side of hub. See **Figure 12**. In most cases, only a slight amount of adjustment is necessary to true rim. After adjustment, rotate rim and make sure another area has not been pulled out of true. Continue adjustment and checking until runout does not exceed 0.08 in. (2mm).

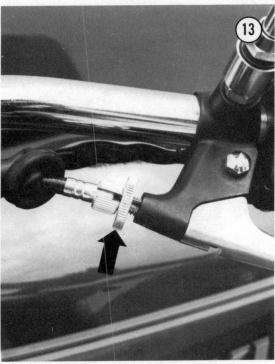

STEERING

Disassembly

1. Place the motorcycle on the centerstand and place a block beneath the engine so the front wheel is held at least ½ in. off the ground.

2. Slacken the clutch cable adjuster (**Figure 13**) and disconnect it from the hand control.

3. Unscrew the master cylinder mounting bolts, remove the mounting clamp, and remove the master cylinder. Unscrew the bolt from the brake hose bracket (**Figure 14**). Temporarily suspend the master cylinder from the right turn indicator; do not allow it to hang by the hose.

4. Unscrew the speedometer and tachometer cables from the instruments.

5. Remove the headlamp lens, unplug the connector, and unscrew the headlamp housing bolts. Remove the housing.

6. Unscrew the bolts that attach the hydraulic manifold to the underside of the bottom triple-clamp (**Figure 15**). Unscrew the brake hose fitting from the caliper and remove the entire brake system.

7. Remove the front wheel as described earlier.

8. Unscrew the bolts from the handlebar clamps (**Figure 16**), remove the clamps, and lay the handlebars on the tank, protected with shop rags.

9. Loosen the pinch bolts in the upper triple-clamp. Unscrew the steering stem bolt (**Fig-**

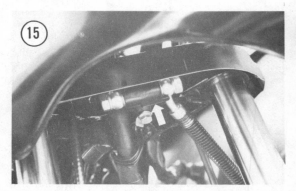

ure 17), loosen the stem pinch bolt, and remove the top triple-clamp.

10. Loosen the bolts in the bottom triple-clamp **(Figure 18)** and pull the forks down and out.

11. Unscrew the steering stem adjusting nut **(Figure 19)**.

12. Place a container under the steering head to catch any ball bearings that might fall and pull the stem down and out.

NOTE: *There are 18 balls in each race.*

Inspection

1. Clean all of the races and the balls with solvent.

2. Check the welds around the steering head for cracks and fractures. If any are found, have them repaired by a competent frame shop or welding service.

3. Check the balls for pitting, scratches, or signs of corrosion. If they are less than perfect, replace them as a set.

4. Check the races for pitting, galling, and cor-

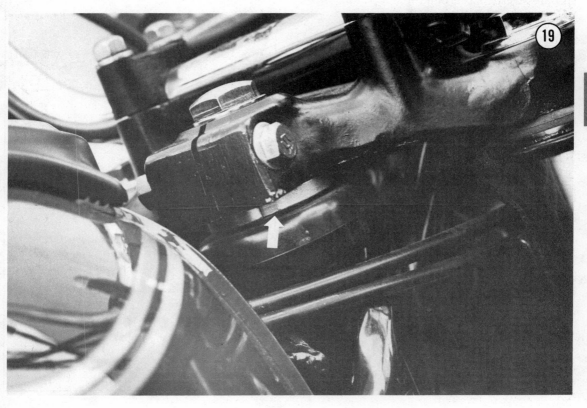

8

rosion. If any of these conditions exist, replace the races. See *Bearing Race Replacement*.

5. Check the steering stem for cracks and check its race for damage or wear. If this race or any of the other races are worn or damaged, they should be replaced as a complete set. Take the old races to your dealer to ensure accurate replacement.

Bearing Race Replacement

1. Insert a hardwood dowel into the steering head **(Figure 20)** and tap around the race to drive it out. Do the same with the opposite race.

2. Install the new races by tapping them into the steering head with a hardwood block **(Figure 21)**. Make sure they are squarely seated in the race bores before tapping them in. Tap them in until they are flush with the steering head.

3. If the steering stem race cannot be removed by hand, pry it up with a screwdriver, working around the circumference of the race, raising it a small amount each time.

4. Install a new stem race by tapping it down progressively, all around the circumference, with a hardwood block.

Assembly

1. Assembly is the reverse of disassembly. Apply a coat of grease to the steering stem to prevent it from rusting.

2. Grease all of the races. Install 18 balls in the steering stem race; they will be held in place by the grease. Install 18 balls in the race in the top of the steering head.

3. Insert the stem into the steering head, hold it in place, and install the top race. Screw on the adjuster nut and tighten it to seat the bearings.

4. Loosen the adjuster until there is play in the stem. Then tighten it just enough to remove both horizontal and vertical play. Check to make sure that the stem will turn from side to side under its own weight, with just a slight push.

5. Continue assembly by following the disassembly steps in reverse. Tighten the lock bolts in the steering stem triple clamp to 1.5-2.5 mkg (11-18 ft.-lb.). Tighten the pinch bolts in the top triple-clamp to 2-3 mkg (9-15 ft.-lb.). Tight-

en the handlebar clamp bolts to 1.2-2 mkg (9-15 ft.-lb.). Tighten them evenly back and forth to maintain equal clearance both front and rear **(Figure 22)**.

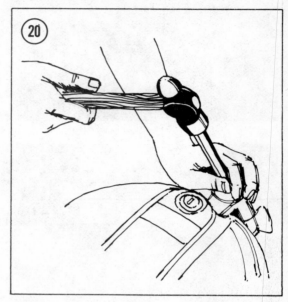

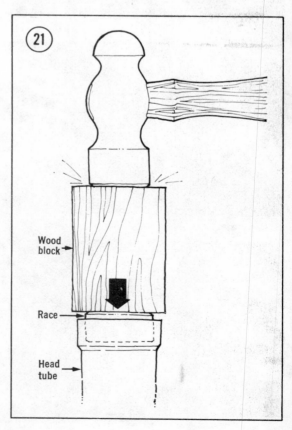

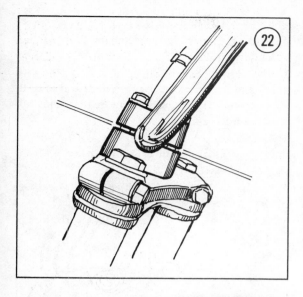

6. When connecting the wires for the directional lamps, connect the light green wire from the harness to the right lamp, and connect the black wire from the harness to the left lamp.

7. When the assembly is complete, refer to Chapter Ten, *Bleeding,* and bleed the brake system before riding the motorcycle.

Steering Head Adjustment

If there is play in the steering stem it may only require adjustment. However, don't take a chance. Disassemble the steering and check for damage or wear that may be the true cause for the play. Adjust the play in the stem as described in Steps 3 and 4 above.

FRONT FORKS

Removal/Installation

1. Remove the front wheel as described under *Front Wheel, Removal/Installation.*

2. Unscrew the caliper mounting bolts (**Figure 23**) and remove the caliper from the fork leg. Suspend it from the directional lamp stalk; don't allow it to hang by the hose.

> NOTE: *On models with twin front disc brakes, remove both calipers if both fork legs are to be removed.*

3. Unscrew the 4 fender mounting bolts and remove the fender.

4. Unscrew the bolts from the handlebar clamps, remove the clamps, and place the handlebars on the fuel tank after protecting it with shop rags.

5. Unscrew the fork cap nuts (**Figure 24**). Loosen the pinch bolts in the top triple-clamp and the lock bolts in the bottom triple-clamp. Pull the fork legs down and out of the clamps.

6. Installation is the reverse of the above. Tighten the pinch bolts in the top triple-clamp to 2-3 mkg (15-21 ft.-lb.). Tighten the lock bolts in the bottom triple-clamp to 1.5-2.5 mkg (11-18 ft.-lb.). Tighten the caliper bolts to 2.5-4 mkg (18-28 ft.-lb.).

Disassembly

> NOTE: *It is not necessary to remove the upper fork legs when routinely servicing*

8

the forks. Much time can be saved by leaving them installed. However, if one or both are damaged, remove them as described above.

1. Remove the handlebars and unscrew the top nuts from the fork legs as described earlier.

2. Unscrew the fork drain plugs and catch the oil in a drip pan.

3. Unscrew the Allen bolt from the bottom of each fork leg (**Figure 25**).

4. Disengage the fork boot from the lower leg and slide it up the upper leg.

5. Pull the lower leg (slider) down and off the upper leg. Disassemble as shown in **Figure 26**.

Inspection

1. Check the sliding surface of the upper fork legs. If they are scuffed and worn, they should be replaced.

2. Check the seals for scratches on their sliding surface and surface them if any are present. Also, replace the seals if leakage was noted before the forks were disassembled.

Seal Replacement

1. Remove the lock ring from the top of the slider (**Figure 27**).

2. Uniformly heat the slider all around the top to expand it. A small propane torch works well for this task. If the slider is not heated, the seal is difficult to remove.

3. Use a large screwdriver and a protector made of soft aluminum (**Figure 28**) to pry out the seal.

4. Clean the seal bore. Coat the circumference of the new seal with assembly oil.

5. Set the seal squarely in the bore with the lip side down (**Figure 29**). Drive the seal in evenly using a ¾ or ⅞ in. socket as a driver until it bottoms in the bore.

Assembly

1. Assembly is the reverse of disassembly (see **Figure 26**). Fill each fork leg with 180cc of a 50/50 mixture of ATF and SAE 10W-30 oil.

2. When the forks are installed, make certain the lip on the dust boot engages the slot in the top of the slider.

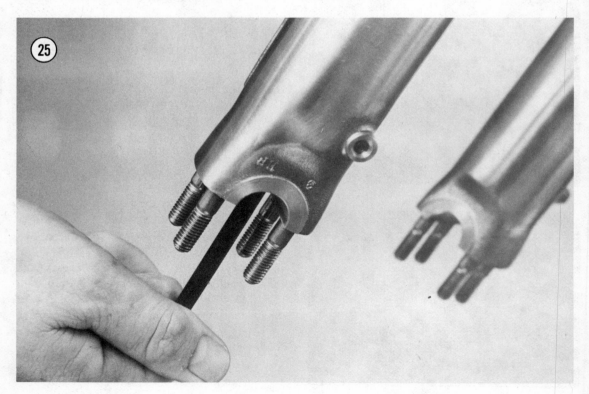

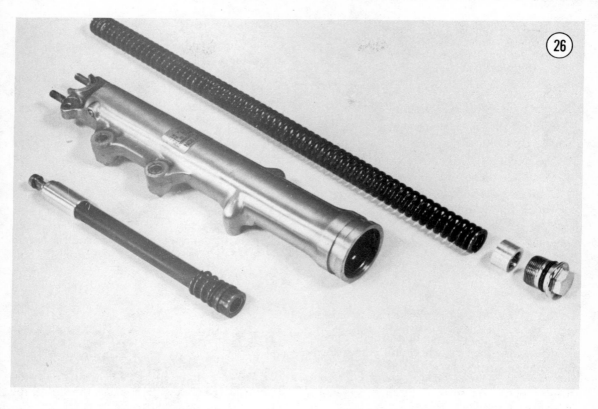

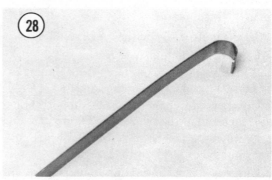

CHAPTER NINE

REAR SUSPENSION

This chapter includes repair and replacement procedures for the rear wheel and rear suspension components.

REAR WHEEL

Removal/Installation

1. Set the motorcycle on the centerstand.

2. Remove the chainguard.

3. Withdraw the lock pin from the right end of the axle (**Figure 1**). Loosen the axle nut.

4. Unscrew the chain adjuster support bolts from each end of the swing arm (**Figure 2**).

5. Remove the cotter key from the brake anchor bolt and unscrew the nut (**Figure 3**).

6. Unscrew caliper mounting bolts (**Figure 4**), lift the caliper off the disc, and suspend it with a piece of cord from the directional light; don't allow the caliper to hang by the hose.

7. Pull back on the rear wheel and swing the chain adjusters down. Push the wheel forward, remove the chain from the sprocket, tilt the top of the wheel to the left (**Figure 5**) and pull it out of the motorcycle.

8. Installation is simply the reverse of this procedure. Before tightening the axle nut, install the caliper and tighten the mounting bolts to 15-21 ft.-lb. (2.3 mkg), and the brake anchor bolt to the same torque. Install a new cotter key

in the brake anchor bolt. Tighten the chain adjuster support bolts. Adjust the chain so there is 0.8-1.2 in. (20-30mm) of free play measured midway between the sprockets (**Figure 6**). Turn the adjusters equally to maintain wheel and chain alignment. Tighten the adjuster locknuts.

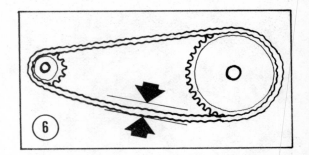

Disassembly

1. Remove the wheel as described above. See NOTE, Step 3, *Inspection*.

2. Pull the drive center out of the hub and collect the spacers (**Figure 7**).

3. Straighten the lock tabs on the carrier bolts (**Figure 8**), unscrew the nuts, and remove the sprocket.

4. Tap the bolts out with a soft mallet, remove the cushion plate (**Figure 9**) and remove the cushion. To remove the disc from the hub, straighten the lock tabs and unscrew the disc mounting bolts.

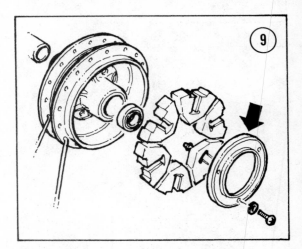

Inspection

1. Rotate the bearings by hand and check for roughness. If the bearings turn smoothly, they

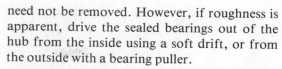

need not be removed. However, if roughness is apparent, drive the sealed bearings out of the hub from the inside using a soft drift, or from the outside with a bearing puller.

2. Check the sprocket for wear and replace it if the teeth show signs of undercutting (**Figure 10**).

3. Measure the thickness of the disc with a micrometer (**Figure 11**). If it is less than 6mm (0.24 in.) thick, replace it. Measure the runout of the disc with a dial indicator (**Figure 12**). If

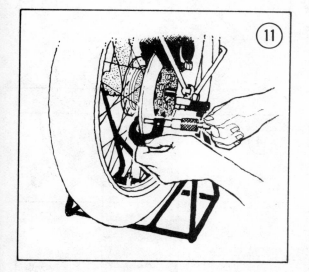

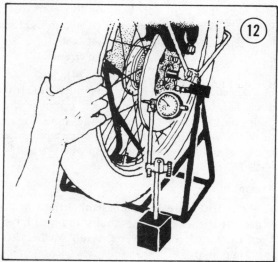

9

runout exceeds 0.3mm (0.012 in.), replace the disc.

> NOTE: *These measurements should be carried out before the wheel is removed from the motorcycle. If the disc is satisfactory, and if it is not scored or discolored from heat, there is no need to remove it from the hub.*

4. Check the axle for straightness (**Figure 13**). If deflection is greater than 0.25mm (0.010 in.), replace the axle.

5. Check for bent, broken, or loose spokes. Replace any that are bent or broken and tighten loose spokes so that all spokes will have an equal "ring" when tapped with a wrench.

6. Check wheel runout (**Figure 14**), it should not exceed 2mm (0.08 in.) at any one point. If it does, carefully tighten the spokes opposite the high point and loosen those on the same side to draw the wheel back on center. Once again, the spokes should have an equal ring when struck.

Assembly

1. Refer to **Figure 15** and assemble the wheel. When the sprocket and disc bolts and nuts have been tightened, bend over the tab washers to lock them in place.

2. Install the wheel as described earlier *(Removal/Installation)* after checking and correcting wheel balance as described below.

Wheel Balancing

An unbalanced wheel can be dangerous. Depending on the degree of unbalance and speed, the rider may experience anything from mild vibration to violent shimmy. In severe cases the rider can lose control.

Wheels are relatively easy to balance without special equipment. Your dealer has an assortment of balance weights which attach to the spokes. They are crimped onto the light side of the wheel with ordinary gas pliers (**Figure 16**). Buy a couple of each weight available (**Figure 17**). If they are undamaged, you can return the unused weights.

> NOTE: *The "adhesive type" balance weights for alloy wheels are available from most auto tire dealers.*

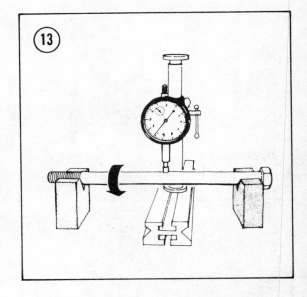

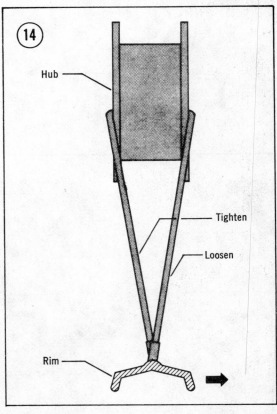

Before balancing the wheel, make sure that the bearings are in good condition and properly lubricated.

1. Support the ends of the axle so the wheel can turn freely (**Figure 18**).

15

REAR HUB ASSEMBLY

1. Brake disc
2. Cover
3. Right spacer
4. Right bearing
5. Internal spacer
6. Hub
7. Left bearing
8. Drive cushion
9. Cushion plate
10. Left spacer
11. Drive plate
12. Left bearing
13. Oil seal
14. Sprocket

16

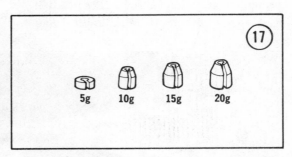

17

5g   10g   15g   20g

18

9

2. Rotate the wheel slowly and allow it to come to rest by itself. Make a chalk mark on the tire at the 6 o'clock position and rotate the wheel as before, several times, noting the position of the chalk mark each time. If it stops at different positions each time, the wheel is balanced.

3. If the chalk mark stops at the same position — 6 o'clock — each time, add weight to the 12 o'clock position until the chalk mark stops at a different position each time.

4. Install the wheel and road test the motorcycle on a smooth, straight road.

SUSPENSION UNITS

The rear suspension units are expendable items; they cannot be rebuilt. If they no longer dampen adequately, they must be replaced, as a set.

Removal/Installation

1. Place the motorcycle on the centerstand and set the spring preload at the softest position.

2. Unscrew the upper and lower mounting bolts and nuts (**Figure 19**) and pull the suspension unit off.

> NOTE: *Remove and install one unit at a time; the unit that remains in place will maintain the correct relationship between the top and bottom mounts and make the job easier.*

3. Installation is the reverse of the above. Tighten the upper mounting nut to 15-21 ft.-lb. (2-3 mkg). Tighten the lower mounting bolt to the same torque value.

SWINGING ARM

The swinging arm pivot is equipped with pressed-in needle bearings. If correctly maintained, with periodic cleaning and greasing, and if the swing arm pivot bolt is kept tight, these bearings should last the life of the motorcycle. However, if they must be replaced, the swinging arm should be removed and entrusted to a dealer; a special puller is required to remove the bearings and it is unlikely that you would ever use it more than once.

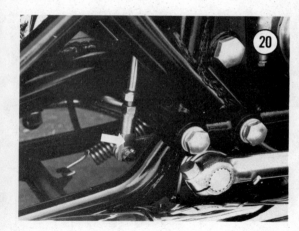

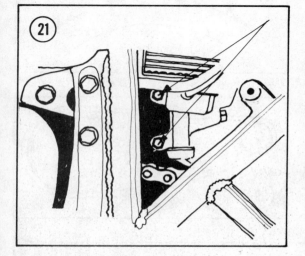

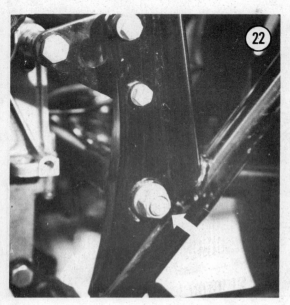

Removal/Installation

1. Disconnect the master cylinder from the brake pedal (**Figure 20**). From the left side, using a long extension, unscrew the bolts that attach the master cylinder to the frame (**Figure 21**).

2. Remove the rear wheel and suspension units as described earlier. Unscrew the nut from the left of the swinging arm (**Figure 22**) and draw the bolt out from the right side. Remove the swinging arm assembly from the frame.

CAUTION
Be careful not to kink the brake line.

3. Disconnect the brake line from the clips at the front and rear of the swinging arm and remove the master cylinder, line, and caliper (**Figure 23**).

4. Remove the end caps and inner bearing races from the swinging arm pivot (**Figure 24**).

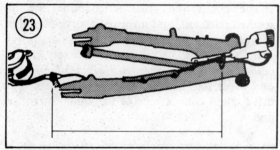

9

5. Check the condition of the needle bearing assemblies (**Figure 25**) and replace them if they are worn or galled, or if they turn with roughness. This is a job for a dealer.

6. Before installing the swinging arm, grease the pivot shaft with a water-proof grease, as well as the bearings, races, and dust caps.

7. Assemble the races and dust caps on the swinging arm, set it in place in the frame, and insert the shaft from the right side. Screw on and tighten the nut. Apply grease, with a gun, through the fitting in the right end of the pivot tube.

DRIVE CHAIN

The drive chain is a long-life, continuous (no master link) type with internal lubrication, between the rollers and pins, sealed in with O-rings. See **Figure 26** for a cross-section of a typical link.

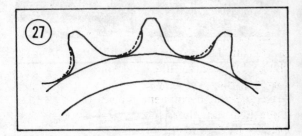

The chain and sprockets, should be inspected, cleaned, and adjusted every 750 miles. If wear on the sprockets or chain rollers is evident, they must be replaced, as a set; *neglect could lead to failure, most likely at high speed, and most likely with dire consequences.* The drive chain cannot receive too much attention and care.

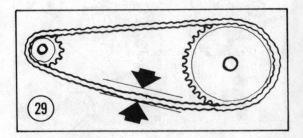

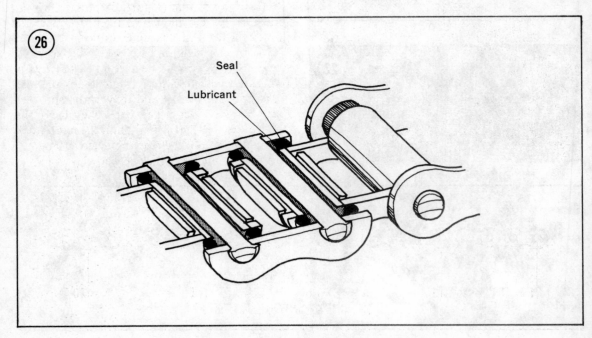

Seal

Lubricant

Cleaning and Lubrication

1. Wash the chain with clean kerosene and dry it thoroughly. This can be done with the chain installed.

CAUTION
Use only kerosene to wash the chain. Do not use gasoline, benzine, or trichloro-ethylene; they will attack the O-ring seals and enter the hermetically sealed, permanently lubricated spaces between the pins and rollers, severely shortening the service life of the chain.

2. Lubricate the outside of the chain with motor oil. Do not use specially compounded chain lubricants; like gasoline and harsh solvents, they will very likely attack the O-ring seals and the permanent lubricant. After the chain has been thoroughly oiled, wipe off the excess with a clean rag.

Inspection

1. Check the sprockets for undercutting of the teeth (**Figure 27**). If wear is evident, replace the sprockets.

2. Measure the chain over a distance of 21 pins (**Figure 28**). If the distance between the pins is greater than 384.8mm (15.1 in.), replace it.

WARNING
Do not attempt to shorten the chain by breaking, removing links, and installing a master link. If this is done, the chain is certain to fail.

Removal/Installation

1. Remove the rear wheel, suspension units, and swinging arm as described earlier. Remove the left rear engine cover to expose the counter-shaft sprocket.

2. Remove the chain and install a new one by reversing the removal procedure. Adjust the new chain so there is free play of 20-30mm (0.8-1.2 in.), measured midway between the sprockets (**Figure 29**).

3. Lubricate the outside of the new chain as described in *Cleaning and Lubrication*.

SPROCKET REPLACEMENT

The rear wheel sprocket replacement is described under *Rear Wheel, Disassembly,* earlier in this chapter. To replace the counter-shaft sprocket, remove the left rear engine cover, straighten the lock tab on the counter-shaft sprocket nut (**Figure 30**), use the rear brake to prevent the wheel from turning, and loosen the nut with an impact driver.

When removing the sprocket, make sure not to remove the spacer behind it. Install a new sprocket engaged with the chain. Lock the rear wheel with the brake and tighten the sprocket nut with an impact driver. Bend one edge of the tab washer over against a flat on the nut to lock it in place. Install the rear engine cover and adjust the chain as described earlier.

9

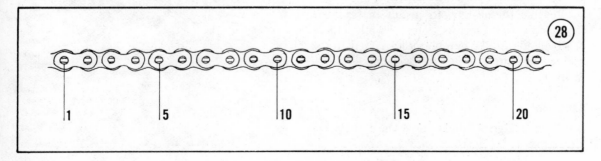

CHAPTER TEN

BRAKES

The GS 750 is equipped with disc brakes on each wheel. The front is operated by a hand lever and the rear is operated by a foot pedal. The front caliper is a single-piston floating caliper type. The rear brake caliper is fixed and has 2 pistons acting in opposition.

Repair and replacement procedures for all brake components are presented in this chapter.

REAR BRAKE CALIPER

Removal/Installation

1. Unscrew the bolt that connects the brake line banjo fitting to the caliper (**Figure 1**). Wrap a rag around the fitting.

2. Remove the cotter key from the brake anchor bolt on the caliper and unscrew the nut and bolt (**Figure 2**).

3. Unscrew the caliper mounting bolts (**Figure 3**) and lift the caliper off the disc.

4. Reverse these steps to install the caliper. Tighten the brake anchor bolt to 2-3 mkg (15-21 ft.-lb.) and install a new cotter key. Tighten the caliper mounting bolts to 2.5-4 mkg (18-29 ft.-lb.).

Diassembly

1. Refer to **Figure 4** and remove the pad inspection cap.

10

2. Remove the stop pins. Press down on the centers of the springs and remove one of the large pins. Relax the springs and remove them. Remove the other large pin and the pads.

3. Unscrew the large Allen bolts and separate the caliper halves.

4. Remove the boot from each piston. Place your hand over a piston and eject it from the caliper with compressed air directed through the internal fluid passage. Do the same with the other caliper half. Remove the O-rings from the cylinders.

Inspection

1. Wash the parts in fresh brake fluid and blow them dry with compressed air.

2. Measure the cylinder bores (**Figure 5**). If either bore is greater than 38.19mm (1.504 in.), the caliper must be replaced.

3. Measure the pistons (**Figure 6**). If either piston is less than 38.13mm (1.501 in.) in diameter, replace them.

4. Inspect the brake pads for wear and replace them if they are worn down to the red indicator line (**Figure 7**).

Assembly

Before beginning assembly of the caliper wash your hands thoroughly with soap and warm water to remove solvent, grease, and buildup of natural body oil.

1. Lubricate new seals with fresh brake fluid and install one in the piston cavity in the inner caliper half (**Figure 8**). Install the other seal in the outer caliper half (**Figure 9**).

2. Install the dust boots on the pistons, making sure the boots are seated in the groove in each piston (**Figure 10**).

3. Lubricate the pistons with fresh brake fluid and install one in the inner caliper half (**Figure 11**) and the other in the outer caliper half (**Figure 12**). Seat the dust boots over the machined shoulders in the caliper.

4. Install the small O-ring in the inner caliper body (**Figure 13**). Assemble the caliper halves, making certain the O-ring remains in place. Screw in and tighten the 2 Allen bolts to 3.5 mkg (25 ft.-lb.).

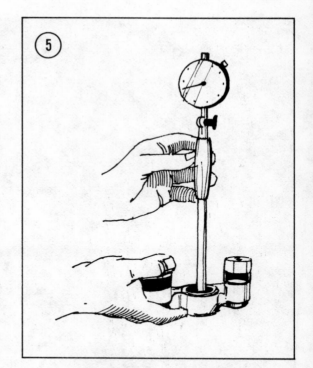

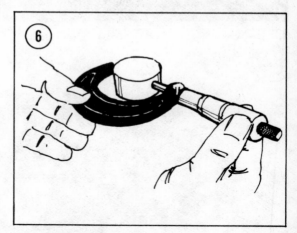

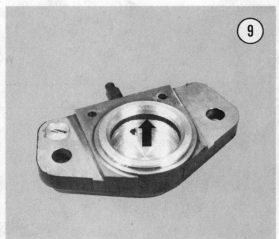

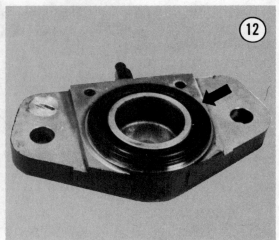

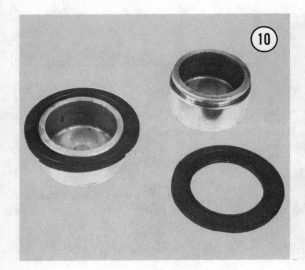

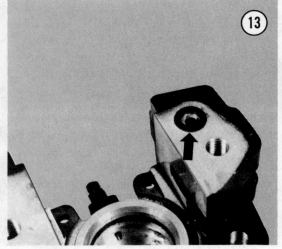

10

5. Install the anti-squeal plates, pads, anti-rattle springs, large pins and stop pins in the caliper. Note that the short end of the anti-squeal plates faces forward. Note also the orientation of the springs; they are located on the outside of each pad, with their center clips over the pads and their ends under the large pins (**Figure 14**).

6. Refer to *Removal/Installation* and install the caliper on the motorcycle. Refer to *Bleeding* and fill and bleed the system.

FRONT BRAKE CALIPER

Removal/Installation

1. Unscrew the bolt that connects the brake line banjo to the caliper (**Figure 15**), place the end of the line in a container, and squeeze the brake lever to expel the fluid. Unscrew the caliper mounting bolts and pull the caliper off the disc.

2. Installation is the reverse of Step 1. Tighten the mounting bolts to 2.5-4.0 mkg (18-28 ft.-

lb.). Tighten the banjo bolt to 1.5-2.5 mkg (11-15 ft.-lb.). Refer to *Bleeding* and fill and bleed the brake system.

Disassembly

1. Refer to **Figure 16** and remove the blanking plugs from the caliper body. Unscrew the screw from the stationary pad, remove the lock plate, and press the pad out of the caliper.

2. Unscrew the caliper bolts and remove the O-rings from them. Remove the sliding plate from the caliper and remove the rubber boots from the raised bosses.

3. Apply air pressure to inlet port in the caliper and eject the piston. Remove the large O-ring from the cylinder.

Inspection

1. Wash the parts in fresh brake fluid and blow them dry with compressed air.

2. Measure the cylinder bore (**Figure 17**). Bore should not exceed 42.89mm (1.69 in.) on single disc models, or 38.23mm (1.51 in.) on dual disc models. If larger, replace the caliper.

3. Measure the piston (**Figure 18**). Diameter must not be less than 42.77mm (1.68 in.) or single disc models, or 38.11mm (1.50 in.) on dual disc models. If less, replace the piston.

4. Inspect the brake pads and replace them if they are worn down to the red indicator line (**Figure 19**).

Assembly

Before beginning assembly of the caliper, wash your hands thoroughly with soap and warm water to remove solvent, grease, and buildup of natural body oil.

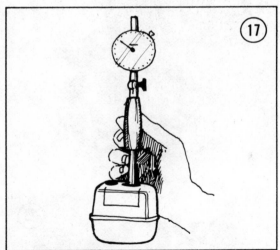

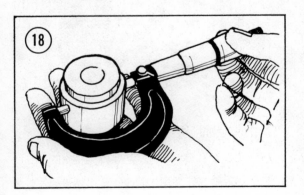

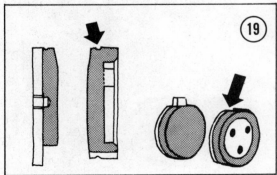

10

1. Lubricate a new seal with fresh brake fluid and install it in the seal groove in the piston cavity in the caliper (**Figure 20**).

2. Lubricate the piston with fresh brake fluid and install it in the cavity (**Figure 21**). Make sure it is square in the bore before pushing it in.

3. Install the dust boot, making sure the seal fits over the shoulder on the caliper and engages the groove in the piston (**Figure 22**). The seal should be lubricated lightly with brake fluid before it is installed. Then, wipe the excess fluid off the outside of the seal so that it will not attract dirt.

4. Lubricate the rubber boots and install them on the bosses of the caliper sliding plate (**Figure 23**).

5. Install the sliding plate in the caliper with the raised, machined bosses *facing* the piston (**Figure 24**). Install new O-rings on the caliper bolts, lubricate them with fresh caliper grease, lock the caliper in a vise with soft jaws, and tighten the bolts to 2.5-3.5 mkg (18-25 ft.-lb.).

6. Apply a light coat of brake pad grease to the back and around the circumference of the sliding pad (No. 1) up to but not beyond the red wear line. Do not get grease on the face of the pad. Line up the groove in the sliding pad with the tab in the caliper and press the pad down against the piston (**Figure 25**).

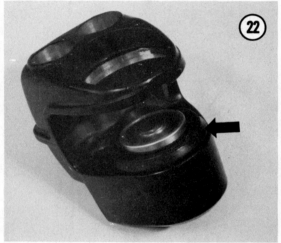

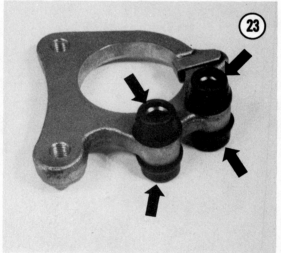

7. Install the stationary pad in the other side of the caliper with the tab on the pad engaged in the slot in the caliper (**Figure 26**). *Do not apply grease to this pad.*

8. Install the pad lock plate and screw and tighten it securely (**Figure 27**).

9. Install the blanking plugs over the caliper bolts (**Figure 28**). Refer to *Removal/Installation* and install the caliper. Refer to *Bleeding* and fill the system with fresh brake fluid and bleed it.

10

MASTER CYLINDERS

The master cylinders are virtually the same internally. They are shown in exploded views in **Figures 29 and 30** for reference. The procedure shown is for the front brake master cylinder. Work on the rear brake master cylinder is much the same.

Removal/Installation — Front

1. Remove the front brake lever. Unscrew the bolts from the clamp that attaches the master cylinder to the handlebar **(Figure 31)**. Unscrew the brake line connector nut from the master cylinder, taking care not to drip fluid onto painted surfaces.

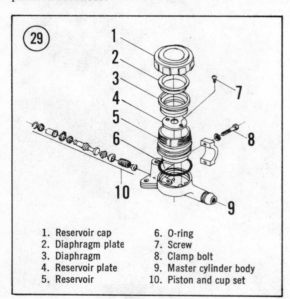

1. Reservoir cap	6. O-ring
2. Diaphragm plate	7. Screw
3. Diaphragm	8. Clamp bolt
4. Reservoir plate	9. Master cylinder body
5. Reservoir	10. Piston and cup set

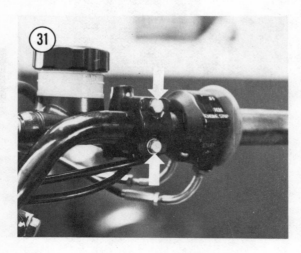

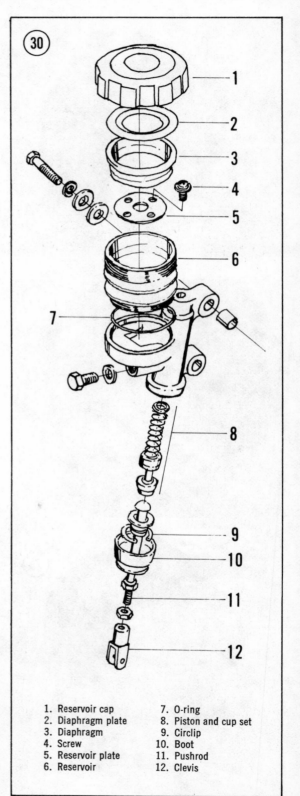

1. Reservoir cap	7. O-ring
2. Diaphragm plate	8. Piston and cup set
3. Diaphragm	9. Circlip
4. Screw	10. Boot
5. Reservoir plate	11. Pushrod
6. Reservoir	12. Clevis

2. Installation is the reverse. Install the brake lever before installing the master cylinder on the handlebar. Maintain a clearance of 2mm ($^3/_{16}$ in.) between the right switch and the master cylinder (**Figure 32**).

3. Reconnect the brake hose oriented as shown in **Figure 33**. Refer to *Bleeding* and fill the system with fresh fluid and bleed it.

Removal/Installation — Rear

1. Disconnect the brake pedal linkage from the master cylinder (**Figure 34**).

2. Unscrew the bolt that attaches the brake line banjo to the top of the master cylinder (**Figure 35**). Take care not to drip brake fluid on painted surfaces.

3. From the left side, with the aid of a long extension, unscrew the bolts that connect the master cylinder to the frame (**Figure 36**). Remove the master cylinder.

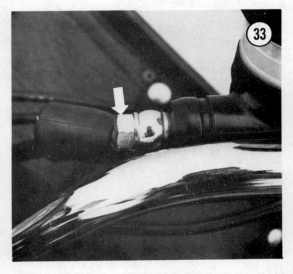

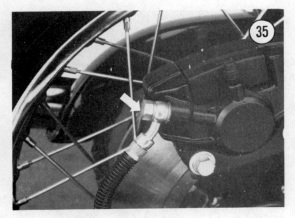

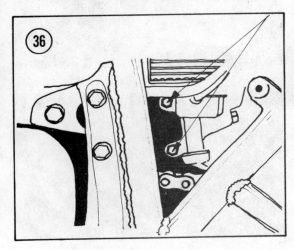

10

4. Installation is the reverse of the preceding steps. Tighten the master cylinder mounting bolts to 1.5-2 mkg (11-15 in.-lb.). Tighten the brake line banjo bolt to 1.5-2.5 mkg (11-18 in.-lb.).

5. Reconnect the brake pedal linkage. Loosen the locknut on the brake pedal stop and screw the stop bolt up until it contacts the mounting plate. See **Figure 37**. Loosen the locknut on the master cylinder pushrod (**Figure 38**) and turn the pushrod until the top of the brake pedal arm is 10mm (0.39 in.) from the bottom of the footrest (**Figure 39**). Tighten the locknut. Run the stop bolt down until there is a clearance of 0.5mm (0.02 in.) between the pedal arm and the stop bolt (**Figure 40**). Tighten the stop bolt locknut and check the free play of the brake pedal. It should be between 9-26mm (0.35-1.00 in.).

Disassembly

1. Remove the snap ring from the end of the master cylinder (**Figure 41**). Special snap ring pliers (Suzuki No. 09920-73110) are shown in use; however. an old pair of long, thin needle-nose pliers can be substituted if their points are bent or filed as shown in **Figure 42**. Remove the reservoir.

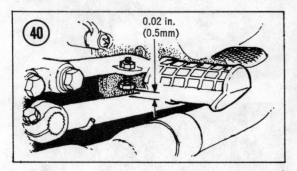

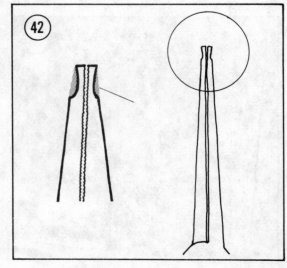

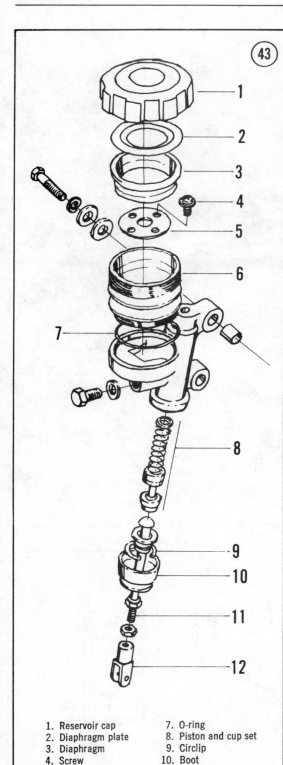

1. Reservoir cap
2. Diaphragm plate
3. Diaphragm
4. Screw
5. Reservoir plate
6. Reservoir
7. O-ring
8. Piston and cup set
9. Circlip
10. Boot
11. Pushrod
12. Clevis

2. Refer to **Figure 43** and disassemble the master cylinder. Discard the pieces shown in **Figure 44**. They are all included in the master cylinder rebuild kit available from Suzuki dealers.

Inspection

1. Wash the master cylinder and reservoir in clean brake fluid and dry them with compressed air.

2. Measure the master cylinder bore. See **Figure 45**. Bore should not exceed 14.05mm (0.553 in.) on single disc models, or 15.93mm (0.63 in.) on dual disc models. Also check the bore for scoring and scuffing. If the bore is too large or there is evidence of damage, replace the master cylinder.

3. Check the O-ring that seals the reservoir and master cylinder amd replace it if it is damaged.

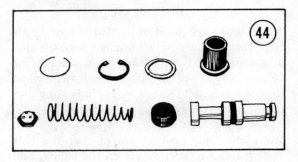

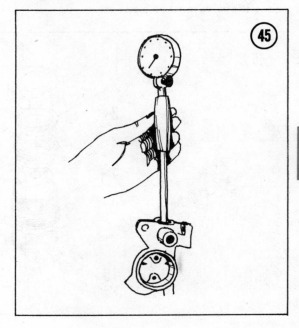

10

Assembly

1. Refer to **Figure 46**. Coat the master cylinder bore with fresh brake fluid. Place all of the internal parts in a shallow container of fresh brake fluid.

2. Assemble the check valve, spring, and primary cup. Install them in the cylinder, making sure the valve and spring do not part and that the primary cup is squarely aligned with the cylinder bore.

3. Install the circlip and rotate it in the groove to make sure it is completely seated.

4. Install the large O-ring in the master cylinder **(Figure 47)**. Install the reservoir and screw in and tighten the 2 screws **(Figure 48)**.

5. Install the master cylinder as described earlier. Refer to *Bleeding* and fill and bleed the system.

BLEEDING

The brake system must be bled to remove air from the cylinders and hydraulic lines each time a line or hose is disconnected, a cylinder or caliper is removed and disassembled, or when the lever or pedal feel is spongy, indicating that there is air in the system.

The procedure is much the same for both front and rear systems except that the rear system has 2 bleeder valves on the caliper and the inside valve must be bled first.

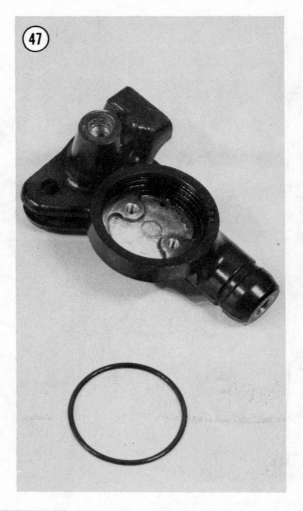

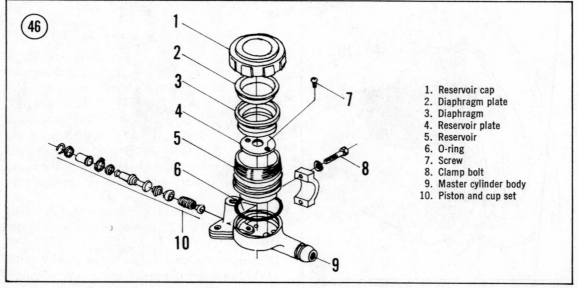

1. Reservoir cap
2. Diaphragm plate
3. Diaphragm
4. Reservoir plate
5. Reservoir
6. O-ring
7. Screw
8. Clamp bolt
9. Master cylinder body
10. Piston and cup set

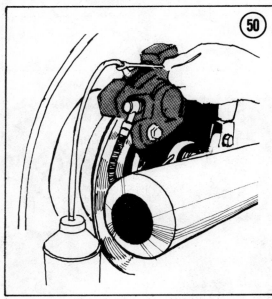

1. Fill the master cylinder reservoir with fresh brake fluid to the LOW line. Install the diaphragm and cap.

WARNING
Use brake fluid marked DOT 3 or SAE J1703 only. Others may vaporize and cause brake failure.

2. Remove the dust cap from the bleeder valve **(Figure 49)** and connect a 2-foot length of clear plastic tubing to the valve. Place the other end of the tubing in a can **(Figure 50)**.

3. Pump the lever or pedal several times until resistance is felt. Hold the lever or pedal down and open the bleeder valve about ¼ turn. Continue to squeeze or press the lever or pedal until it stops. Hold it in this position and close the bleeder valve.

4. Release the lever or pedal and repeat the previous step as many times as necessary until the fluid passing through the hose is free of air bubbles.

NOTE: *Do not allow the reservoir to empty during bleeding or more air will be drawn into the system, requiring it to be bled completely once again.*

5. When the fluid is free of air, tighten the bleeder valve, remove the hose, and install the dust cap. Hold the lever or pedal down tightly and check the connections for leaks. Correct any that are found. Fill the reservoir to the FULL mark and install the diaphragm and cap tightly.

CHANGING BRAKE FLUID

Each time the reservoir cap is removed for inspection of the brake fluid level a small amount of dirt and moisture enters the reservoir. The same thing occurs if there is a leak, or any part of the system is loosened or disconnected. Dirt can clog the system or cause rapid wear of the cylinders and pistons. Water in the fluid vaporizes at high temperature, impairing hydraulic action and reducing brake performance.

For these reasons it is essential that the fluid be changed every 2 years to ensure peak brake performance.

1. Remove the dust cap from the bleeder valve of the brake being drained and connect a length

10

of hose to the valve. Place the other end of the hose in a container (**Figure 50**).

2. Remove the cap and diaphragm from the master cylinder.

3. Open the bleeder valve ½ turn and repeatedly operate the brake lever or pedal until fluid is no longer expelled. Close the bleeder valve.

4. Fill and bleed the system as described under *Bleeding*.

> *WARNING*
> *Do not reuse the fluid that was drained or that was passed through the system during bleeding. Discard it.*

BRAKE DISC

The brake discs should be routinely inspected every 3,000 miles for scoring, abrasion, and runout. If the disc is scored or grooved deep enough to snag a fingernail, it should be replaced.

Check disc runout with a dial indicator. Raise the wheel being checked and set the arm of a dial indicator against the surface of the disc (**Figure 51**) and slowly rotate the wheel while watching the indicator. If runout is greater than 0.3mm (0.012 in.), replace the disc.

Measure the thickness of the disc with a micrometer at 8 locations around the disc. If the thickness of the disc is less than 6mm (0.24 in.) on single disc models, or 5.5mm (0.22 in.) on dual disc models, replace it.

Removal/Installation

1. Refer to Chapter Eight *(Front Suspension)*, or Chapter Nine *(Rear Suspension)* and remove the wheel.

2. Straighten the lock tabs on the disc bolts (**Figure 53**). Unscrew the bolts and remove the disc.

3. When installing the disc, tighten the bolts to 1.5-2.5 mkg (11-18 ft.-lb.). Bend a lock tab over against one flat on each bolt.

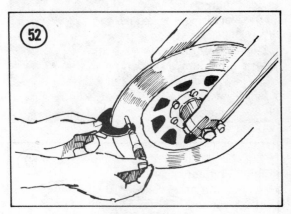

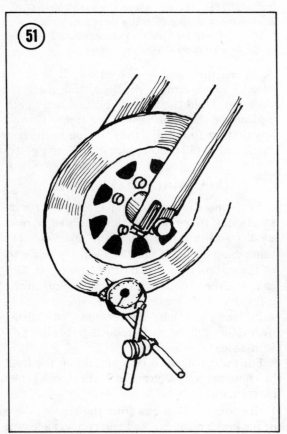

CHAPTER ELEVEN

PERFORMANCE IMPROVEMENT

While the Suzuki GS750 is an impressive high-performance machine in stock configuration, for many riders stock isn't enough.

High-performance building, particularly with the GS750, will do a great deal to make an already fine motorcycle even better.

With minimum modifications, stock horsepower may be doubled, and handling, braking, and suspension may be markedly improved for any use, whether it be high-speed touring, production road racing or street/strip drag racing.

Too many riders consider high performance nothing but hotrodding the engine. However, an equal amount of attention must be paid to the suspension and braking, to make sure that the bike's capabilities remain equal.

With most Japanese bikes, the first area of concern should be better handling rather than more horsepower. However, the GS750, in stock configuration, is a superb handling machine. Very few modifications are needed to make the suspension exceptional in any application, up to and including full-tilt production road racing.

Since high-performance accessories require time for research, development, tooling, and production after a model is introduced, some time must pass before total performance packages are available. Since the GS750 is a newcomer to the market, performance accessories were still being introduced as this book went to press. So, if a product is not mentioned in this chapter, it may well not have been available in time.

Another problem which frequently occurs when a new model machine is being built for performance is the discovery of weak points. A given component in an engine may be sufficiently strong for stock application. But when horsepower is radically increased, that part may fail. With a new model, this problem may be compounded by the unavailability of a more durable replacement.

PLANNING PERFORMANCE

Before you begin spending money in all directions for high-performance parts, the first step is to plan what you want as an end product.

If only minor improvements are needed, it is financially unwise to spend a thousand dollars or more for major engine building. If the bike will be ridden two-up with touring gear, there is little point in tuning the suspension for cafe racing.

Once you figure out what you want as an end product, the parts and work may be done in stages. Working step by step is not only the soundest budgetary way to build a bike, but it will ensure that each improvement gives the most benefits at the time it's put on, rather than being a help five stages later.

The first step, of course, is to keep a machine highly tuned and maintained at all times to get the most from stock. For example, a poorly maintained, worn, and misadjusted chain may rob as much as 10-20% of available horsepower. Another particularly important area on all multi-carb, multi-cylinder machines is carburetor synchronization. Far too many shop mechanics will roughly synchronize the carburetors, rather than make sure they are exactly set. Also, very few of the multi-carb setups will stay synchronized beyond 500 miles. For this reason, it is very important to spend the money for a set of vacuum gauges or Carb-Stix from Gerex, and do the work yourself.

CARBURETOR TUNING TIPS

Three models of carburetors are found on the GS750. Type One is found on model numbers 10001-11346 and 12357-12417, and Types Two or Three (internally identical), on all other models.

Type One differs from the later models in having a fixed air jet. Base line jetting for all three models may be found in **Table 1**.

Table 1
BASELINE CARBURETOR JETTING

Fitting	Type One	Type Two & Three
Main jet	105	97.5
Needle jet	P1	06
Throttle valve	2.5	1.5
Pilot jet	22.5	27.5
Air jet	Fixed 1.1	0.7
Air jet screw	1¼ turns out	1¾ turns out
Fuel jet screw	1¼ turns out	⅜ turn out

A slight hesitation on acceleration may be experienced on any GS750. This may be fixed on models with Type One carburetors by changing the jetting to that in **Table 1**, and then modifying the main jet to meet local riding conditions.

On machines equipped with Type Two or Three carburetors, the hesitation may be cured by replacing the 27.5 pilot jet with a 15 pilot jet, the 97.5 main jet with a 100 main jet, and adjusting the air jet screw out 1 turn, the fuel jet screw out 1 turn. See **Figure 1**. It is extremely important that when adjusting the air or fuel screws, they be screwed in gently until they seat.

CAUTION
Do not bottom them out or the seats will be ruined and the entire carburetor body will have to be replaced.

ENGINE BUILDING

Exhaust

Increasingly restrictive noise laws have made all motorcycle manufacturers radically muffle their bikes. Stock exhaust systems are designed for maximum horsepower, consistent with the legal sound level limits.

Replacement of the stock exhaust with a four-into-one (**Figure 2**) header system will markedly increase power (about 0.2 seconds in quarter mile elapsed time). This will be at the expense of slightly increased noise output, although it need not be to an excessively obnoxious or illegal degree. The problem is to choose an exhaust system which will actually offer

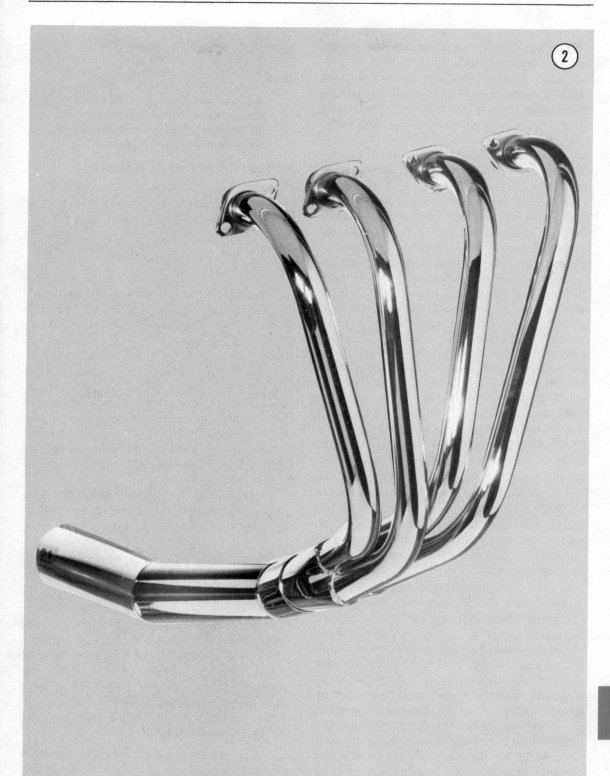

more power rather than just more noise, as far too many accessory systems do. Since all manufacturers advertise that their pipes add performance, whereas very few actually do, the best way to pick a system is at the drag strip. A little research among the riders of consistently winning bikes will show which systems work, even muffled for street use. Among these power-producing systems are those from RC Engineering, Kerker, MTC Engineering, and Yoshimura R&D.

Various other exhaust systems are offered, including 4 separate drag pipes, four-into-two systems, and optional mufflers which fit the existing header pipes. While these exhaust systems may be stylish and useful in certain applications (such as touring with saddlebags), none of them seem to have been the choice for serious competitors, and the performance-oriented rider should allow for this.

Once the exhaust system is installed, it will be necessary to rejet the carburetors. Normally the only change required is to increase the main jet about 5 points (one size), and possibly, to raise the needle position one notch.

To determine what rejetting requirements will be, take a high-speed plug reading. On a deserted road, accelerate to 5000 rpm, and hold for $1/8$-$1/4$ mile. Chop the throttle, cut the kill button and pull in the clutch. Drift the bike to a halt and remove the plugs. They should indicate a slightly lean condition. Install the larger jets and take another reading. On the Suzuki, when a performance exhaust is installed, it may be necessary to increase the main jet two sizes to get a correct reading.

When a high-performance exhaust system is installed on a GS750 equipped with the Type One carburetors, severe exhaust pipe bluing will almost certainly occur. This is uncorrectable, due to the fixed air jet in the carburetors. While unpleasant looking, it should not be regarded as significant or dangerous.

Exhaust systems which purport to offer increased power, with no carburetor rejetting necessary, should be regarded skeptically. Obviously if no rejetting is necessary, no improvement in the exhaust flow has been made, and the only benefit gained from such an exhaust system will be a reduction in the weight of the bike.

CAUTION
Open, unmuffled exhausts should not be run on the street under any circumstances. It is extremely bad for the image of all motorcyclists, and could well lead to stringent anti-motorcycle legislation. In addition, just uncorking the exhausts will not increase power and may lead to severe engine damage.

Big Bore Kits

The least expensive and most noticeable improvement in engine performance will come from increasing the displacement. This will add power throughout the engine's rpm range, yet will have no other drawbacks than slightly decreased gas mileage.

A number of multi-cylinder machines require reinforcement of many of the lower end components (crank, connecting rods, bearings) before big bore kits may be installed. However, the GS750's lower end is more than strong enough to take any of the kits currently available on the market. The connecting rods will take horsepower more than twice stock rating without breakage. The press-fit crankshaft requires no welding of the throws to prevent movement, due to the serrated edges on the throws. All engine modifications may be done without tearing down the engine or transmission.

Big bore kits are currently available from three manufacturers, in several different configurations.

Yoshimura R&D's 850 Kit

This includes cast pistons, wrist pins, retainers, rings, and a new head gasket (**Figure 3**). The stock cylinder sleeve must be bored by an experienced automotive or motorcycle machine shop to accept the new 69mm domed pistons which will increase engine displacement to 845cc's. Compression is raised to 10:1, so premium gas must be used in this engine (as in all of the big bore kits currently available).

RC Engineering's 870 Kit

Again, this kit requires boring of the stock sleeves to new dimensions, in this case 70mm. Compression goes up to 10.8:1, which is just about the maximum which may be used with to-

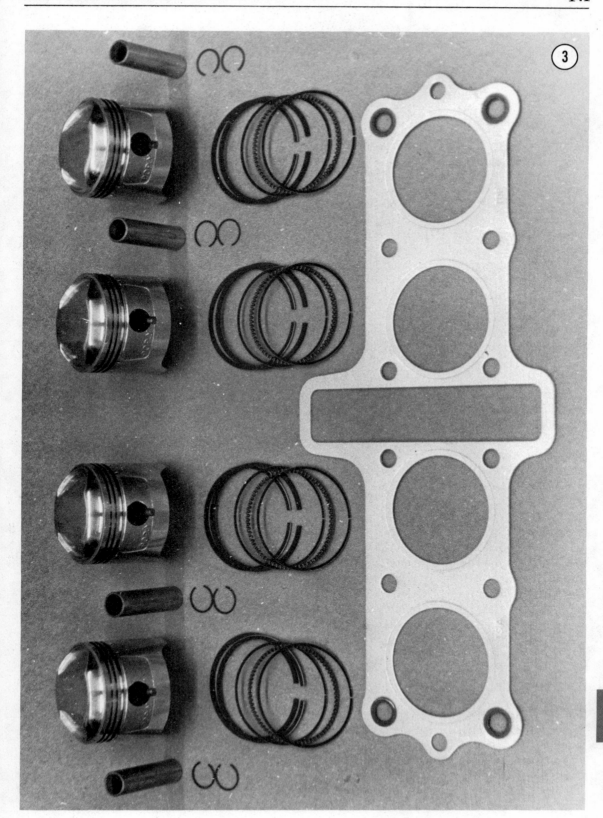

day's "premium" gasoline. Pistons are forged rather than cast, which means that piston-cylinder wall clearance must be greater than with cast pistons.

MTC Engineering

Three kits are available from MTC Engineering: the 780cc kit using new 67mm pistons, the 870 kit with 70mm pistons and the largest kit currently on the market, 920cc's, using 72mm pistons. The smaller kits may be installed after the stock liner is rebored, but the 920 kit requires resleeving the cylinders. This work should only be done by an experienced motorcycle performance shop and is not a job for the inexperienced mechanic. MTC will handle the modification by mail order at a reasonable price.

With a big bore kit installed, power will be increased around 25-30%, and should reduce quarter mile times to between 11.9-12.2 with no other modifications.

High compression pistons (**Figure 4**) are available with all of these kits (generally around 12:1), but should not be used on a GS750 intended for street use. Super high compression will add a small amount of horsepower in the midrange, nothing at all to the top end, and will seriously increase engine heat and consequent wear. It is almost impossible to find pump gasoline with an octane rating high enough to allow this high a compression ratio.

With significantly increased displacement, stock carburetion will be inadequate. Until you can afford high-performance carburetors, the stock carburetors may be rejetted. Base line jetting for a big bore kit will probably involve an increase of the main jet diameter by two sizes, and the jet needle moved up one notch.

Carburetion

Carburetor performance may be improved in one of two ways — either by replacement or by increasing the venturi size of the stock carburetors.

The least expensive modification (around $100) is to bore the stock 26mm carburetors to 29mm. This work may be done by any good motorcycle speed shop (dirt-racing shops are generally quite familiar with this modification) or by mail order from RC Engineering.

If mail ordered, the carburetors will be returned prejetted to a full rich position, with the needle position in the top notch and the main jet size up two sizes from stock. Adjustment of the needle and possibly another change to the main jet should be the only jetting changes necessary after the carburetors are installed on the bike. It will not be necessary to modify the cutaway or any other part on the bored-out carburetors for them to work correctly.

With these carburetors, power will be significantly increased. However, mileage will drop severely (by more than five miles to the gallon).

A better solution, although more expensive (around $300), is to replace the stock carburetors with a set of 29mm smoothbore Mikunis. These lightweight aluminum-bodied carburetors are very similar to the stockers in appearance (**Figure 5**), but offer heavy (10-12%) performance boosts.

Power increases will be most noticeable through midrange and on the top end when the 29mm smoothbores are installed. In addition, the carburetors usually increase mileage, by as much as two to three miles to the gallon, even when installed on a large-displacement engine.

These carburetors are sold premounted on a conventional linkage block, and require about 15 to 20 minutes to install on a bike. They are closely prejetted, and should require little setting after installation. A peculiarity of the smoothbores, however, is that when they are correctly jetted, a slightly lean condition will be indicated on taking a plug reading.

Camshafts

After the big bore kit, exhaust and carburetors have been fitted to the engine, the next stage is to replace the stock camshafts. Once again, due to the newness of the GS750, very few options are available. Most of the cams now on the market, such as those sold by MTC Engineering (produced by Kenny Harmon) are regrinds of stock shafts. Due to delays in billet production, the only all-new billet camshafts are those made by Yoshimura R&D (**Figure 6**).

11

These camshafts are stock Suzuki billet blanks, which are bought in Japan and then ground to meet Yoshimura's specifications.

Two different sets are available from Yoshimura. The first, which increases lift and duration from stock, is intended for use on street or street/strip bikes. With this set of cams, power will be increased throughout the engine's rpm range.

For racing, the Yoshimura Stage II cams should be used. Since these are intended to produce maximum power in the upper rpm ranges, they aren't practical for street use.

Both of these camshaft sets are drop-in; installed in the same manner as the stock shafts, and require no modification to the heads. Valve springs should, however, be replaced with S&W heavy duty springs (available from Yoshimura).

Headwork

Head design is the biggest single factor in the GS750's rather amazing stock performance. However, this may be further improved by a custom porting job (**Figure 7**).

It should be emphasized that cleanup, porting, and matching of combustion chambers should not be done by the amateur mechanic, as head damage is more likely to result than is improved performance. Headwork should be done *only* by an experienced motorcycle porting service such as Branch Flowmetrics, RC Engineering, Yoshimura R&D, or MTC Engineering.

Porting may be done not only to generally improve performance throughout the powerband, but to change the characteristics for a given application (such as Bonneville racing, road racing, etc.). With a custom porting job intended for street use, power will be upped 10-15%, and mileage and valve train life will also be increased.

If the bike is to be used in competition, the valve train may be further modified. Yoshimura R&D will replace the stock valves with stainless steel parts having smaller-than-stock stems. These, coupled with reduced ID guides, will reduce valve train interia and enable the engine to rev higher and more quickly.

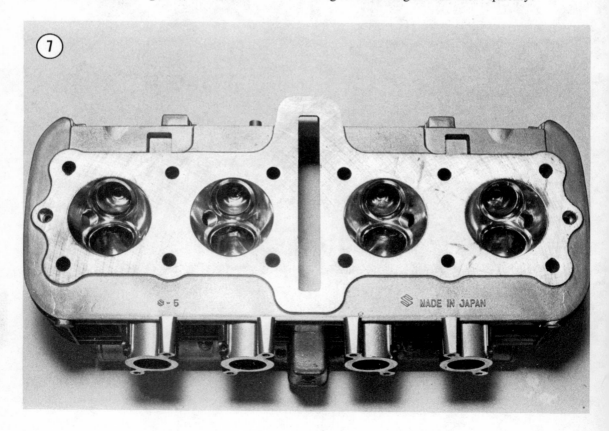

The stock valve adjustment cups and shims are replaced with lightweight cups and very small shims **(Figure 8)**. The shims are installed directly on the valve stem, and the caps over them. The camshafts then work directly on the caps. These parts are intended for use on a high-revving engine, and will eliminate the possibility of the stock shims being flung out at high rpm. However, when this system is installed, it will be necessary to remove the cam-shafts to adjust the valves.

The cam chain is replaced with a Yoshimura heavy-duty chain, and the automatic cam chain tensioner is replaced with a manual tensioner **(Figure 9)**. A small metal plate is fitted to the rubber cam chain tensioner spring, to prevent the new manual adjuster from wearing through the rubber spring facing **(Figure 10)**. None of these modifications are considered necessary for street performance.

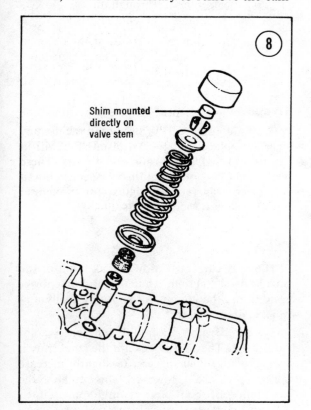

Shim mounted directly on valve stem

11

Oil Cooler

With a larger displacement, high compression engine, heat will increase. Installation of an oil cooler will significantly increase engine life.

However, since there are no external lines on the GS750 which may be used to easily fit an oil cooler, it will be necessary to remove the oil pressure switch fitting and install a fitting with hose mounts **(Figure 11)**. Such a fitting is available separately from Yoshimura R&D, or as a complete kit, including cooler, from Lockhart Industries. Using the Yoshimura fitting, an oil cooler must be procured separately (Lockhart being highly recommended) and mounted to the frame just below the steering head.

Ignition

Stock ignition systems are generally acceptable only for stock applications. When a performance machine is built and ridden hard, problems with the system will occur. These may include points bounce (and consequent ignition miss) at high rpm, loss of power at high rpm, and insufficient spark.

The Suzuki GS750's ignition may be markedly improved by replacing the stock ignition coils with replacement dual-wire coils from Andrews Products **(Figure 12)**. These increase voltage output to 30,000 volts.

Still greater benefits are possible by replacing the entire stock ignition system with a Gerex CDI (actually an electronically-triggered battery-coil system). Not only can the Gerex be set once and sealed up, but performance will also be slightly increased, particularly at high rpm.

Other electronic ignition systems on the market have shown little power increase; their main advantage is that they are set-and-forget systems.

Turbocharging

Since the GS750's lower end is extremely sturdy, a bolt-on performance package is American Turbo-Pak's turbocharger kit **(Figure 13)**.

Fitted to an otherwise stock engine, 1-1½ seconds will be cut from the quarter mile elapsed time figures. Installation of the kit requires removal of the stock exhaust and carburetors, and installation of the turbo in its place. The turbocharger uses a single Bendix carburetor, and is driven by exhaust gases.

Turbocharging should be considered as a performance boost for use by an experienced rider on a strip or short-trip street machine, rather than as a universal performance modification. Turbocharging, if properly set up for street riding, will offer performance boosts at high rpm only. At low and normal riding ranges, the bike will have stock performance only. Secondly, a turbocharger operates at high engine temperatures — something to be avoided for the long distance street rider.

Transmission

Riders building GS750's for road racing may wish to replace the stock transmission with a Yoshimura R&D close-ratio set of gears. These heavy-duty parts are drop-in replacements, and will offer gear ratios designed for maximum power useage at racing speeds.

Clutch

The only currently-known weak point of the Suzuki is its clutch. Under high-horsepower conditions, the clutch will slip very easily and quickly destroy itself.

Two moderately acceptable temporary solutions exist. The first is to shim the stock clutch springs with 0.060 spacers, to slightly increase spring pressure. However, this creates the possibility of coil bind, troublesome clutch disengagement on a cold engine and also, markedly increases clutch lever force.

A second solution is to replace the entire stock clutch pack with a set of fiber and metal plates from a Honda 360 twin. These heavier plates will eliminate slippage, but with the drawback of slight clutch hangup when the engine is cold.

The best solution is to replace the clutch with a heavy duty kit from Barnett Tool & Engineering.

Yoshimura R&D and RC Engineering are also developing heavy-duty clutch kits for the GS750 which should be on the market in a fairly short time.

HANDLING

The GS750 is unique among Japanese multi-cylinder machines in being, in stock trim, a motorcycle with excellent handling characteristics.

Even for full-on competition, very few modifications need to be made.

However, some improvements may be made even for normal street use. Since the GS750 has no major handling problems, these improvements should best be made when stock components wear out. At that time, high-performance parts should be used for replacement items.

Front Forks

While relatively precise in handling, the Suzuki's front forks are sprung quite softly for high-speed riding or for proper suspension when a full-size touring fairing is installed. An inexpensive improvement is to add one inch spacers inside the forks, above the springs (**Figure 14**). These spacers should have a diameter matching the spring diameter.

A more sophisticated improvement is to replace the stock fork springs and shock cylinder with S&W heavy-duty parts. These will stiffen the front end and provide more precise damping behavior, particularly under hard cornering. In addition, the S&W parts will have a life expectancy far longer than stock components.

Rear Shocks

When the stock shock absorbers wear out, they should be replaced with S&W air shocks. These shocks use an air reservoir, contained in an expandable rubber casing to replace the normal springs. Damping is conventionally handled with an oil reservoir.

Air shock mounting is simple, and requires replacing the old shocks with the new parts, connecting two air lines to the shocks, and then interconnecting the air lines to a common T-airfitting, which may be mounted through a sidecover.

Once mounted, some experimentation must be made with air pressure to find the desired ride, although 30-35 psi is generally optimum for high-performance riding.

Care must be taken to ensure that the air shocks are adequately clearanced from chain guard, saddlebags, rear disc, etc., since the rubber reservoir expands considerably under compression (**Figure 15**). With the air shocks installed, the bike will sit about one inch lower than stock at the rear.

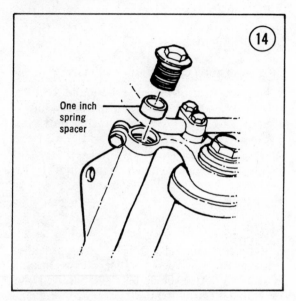

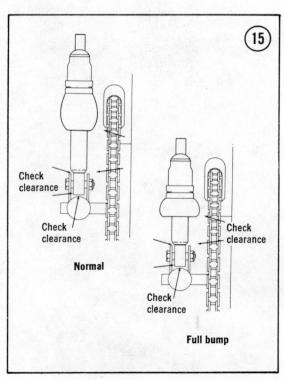

The advantage of air shocks is their almost infinite adjustability. They may be set quite rigidly for drag strip use, less firm for mountain road riding (or production racing), or quite soft for long distance touring. Life expectancy from the S&W air shocks will be upwards of 50,000 miles.

For those who want more conventional rear shocks, S&W or Koni shocks are excellent replacement items.

Swingarm and Frame Modifications

No modifications need to be made to either the stock swingarm or frame for any kind of street riding. For production racing, however, two crossbraces may be added to the frame — one between the frame forward downtubes just below the engine cylinders, and another between the frame toptubes near the seatpost area (**Figure 16**).

Wheels

Reducing unsprung weight — unsuspended parts of the bike such as wheels, tires, brakes, etc. — will improve any bike's handling. However, this is certainly not necessary for any kind of street riding, since the benefits will not be ex-

perienced until close-to-the-limit conditions are reached.

The stock wheels may be replaced with Akront or DID rims for weight reduction purposes. At a greater expense, cast alloy wheels may be used (**Figure 17**), with those from either Morris Industries, Lester Wheel or Performance Machine (modified U.S. mag-style wheels) particularly recommended.

Use of cast alloy wheels will generally slightly reduce unsprung weight. But their main recommendations are: increased rigidity, which markedly increases tire life and improves handling through less side stress distortion; the deep dish design which reduces the possibility of spinning a tire off of the rim after a blowout; and less maintenance (no spokes to be adjusted).

All three of the mentioned wheels are bolt-on replacement items, and may either use the stock Suzuki's brake system or optional high-performance braking systems.

Brakes

The stock discs may be removed and lightened. This is done by facing the disc on a lathe down to about ⅔ of its stock width. However, this cutting must be done by an *experienced*

16

brake specialist, since it is extremely easy to "chunk" the disc during cutting and ruin it. Most road racing- oriented shops can provide this service. Further lightening may be done by drilling holes in the disc (**Figure 18**). Again, this is not an amateur operation, since the holes must be slightly countersunk to prevent puck damage. Drilled discs will not only be quite lighter, but also will provide far better stopping performance in the rain.

Plasma-coated light alloy replacement discs may be ordered from Performance Machine, for around $90 each.

The addition of a second front disc brake to high-performance motorcycles is quite popular. However, the GS750 forks are only tabbed to mount a caliper on one leg. To run dual discs, it will be necessary to buy a second left fork leg, and install that in place of the right one. The new caliper will then be mounted facing forward. A more aesthetic, and far more expensive, way is to replace the stock front end with a set of 38mm Ceriani road racing forks. This modification will also require replacing the stock headlight, fabricating brackets for the gauges, and is hardly recommended for the street rider.

Many riders find that the rear disc on the GS750 is entirely too sensitive, particularly for high-speed riding. An easy solution is to install a Safety Braker on the rear caliper. See **Figure 19**. This will reduce line pressure under hard braking, and make the rear disc almost impossible to lock up.

Tires

High-performance street tires are inevitably a compromise between a compound hard enough to provide acceptable tire life, and one soft enough to give sufficient adhesion.

While the Dunlop K-series and Goodyear high-performance tires are excellent, probably the best street performance tires available today are from Continental. While expensive, they provide the maximum adhesion for high-speed road riding and still have an acceptable lifespan. For the long range touring rider, the Michelin M45 tires will give extraordinary lifespan at the slight expense of maximum adhesion.

Overall

Properly built, maintained and tuned, the Suzuki GS750 can offer double the stock horsepower and still be a reliable and nontemperamental machine. It is the first generation of the new "superbikes" — a motorcycle not only with an engine that is extraordinarily powerful and sturdy, but a bike which was designed and constructed to handle and brake as well.

11

Table 2   HIGH PERFORMANCE ACCESSORY MANUFACTURERS

Company	Service
American Turbo-Pak, Inc. 2127 S. Hathaway Santa Ana, Calif. 92705	Turbochargers
Andrews Products, Inc. 9872 Farragut St. Rosemont, Ill. 60018	High performance coils
Branch Flowmetrics 2625 Lime Ave. Long Beach, Calif. 90806	Porting, headwork
G&O Manufacturing 78 Lake Meadow Dr. Daly City, Calif. 94015	Safety Braker
Gerex 2711 Toledo, #105 Torrance, Calif. 90503	Electronic ignition, Carb-Stix
The Lester Tire & Wheel Co. 26881 Cannon Road Bedford Heights, Ohio 44146	Cast alloy wheels
Lockhart Industries, Inc. 15707 Texaco Ave. Paramount, Calif. 90723	Oil coolers
Morris Industries 2901 W. Garry Ave. Santa Ana, Calif. 92704	Cast alloy wheels, disc brakes
MTC Engineering 5204 Chakemco St. South Gate, Calif. 90280	Big bore kits, cams, porting
Performance Machine 16248 Minnesota Paramount, Calif. 90723	Cast alloy wheels, disc brakes
Racecrafters International 7801 Canoga Ave. Canoga Park, Calif. 91304	Kerker exhausts, Mikuni smoothbore carbs
RC Engineering 16216 S. Main St. Gardena, Calif. 90248	Exhausts, Mikuni smoothbore carbs, big bore kits, porting, headwork engine building
S&W Engineered Products 2617 W. Woodland Dr. Anaheim, Calif. 92801	Air shocks, front fork springs, fork kits
Yoshimura R&D 5517 Cleon Ave. N. Hollywood, Calif. 91601	Cams, big bore kits, exhausts, headwork, engine building

11

INDEX

12